coaching.

Jan balances a busy and challenging working life
with travel, adventure, friendship and fun.

She can be contacted at
jan@janfergusontraining.co.uk

## OTHER TITLES IN THE SERIES

# PERFECT
# ASSERTIVENESS

### All you need to get it right first time

## Jan Ferguson

RANDOM HOUSE

BUSINESS BOOKS

3 5 7 9 10 8 6 4

This edition published in the United Kingdom in 2003
by Random House Business Books

First published in 1996 by Arrow Books
Random House, 20 Vauxhall Bridge Road, London SW1V 2SA

Random House Australia (Pty) Limited
20 Alfred Street, Milsons Point
Sydney, New South Wales 2061, Australia

Random House New Zealand Limited
18 Poland Road, Glenfield
Auckland 10, New Zealand

Random House South Africa (Pty) Limited
Endulini, 5a Jubilee Road, Parktown 2193, South Africa

Random House UK Limited Reg. No. 954009

ISBN 1844131548

Companies, institutions and other organizations wishing to make
bulk purchases of any business books published by Random House
should contact their local bookstore or Random House direct:
Special Sales Director
Random House, 20 Vauxhall Bridge Road, London SW1V 2SA

Tel: 0171 840 8470 Fax: 0171 828 6681

www.randomhouse.co.uk
businessbooks@randomhouse.co.uk

Typeset in Sabon by SX Composing DTP, Rayleigh, Essex
Printed and bound in Great Britain by Bookmarque Ltd, Croydon

For Lucy and Rosie . . .
my gold.

# Contents

# Acknowledgements

Thank you to my husband Malcolm who probably doesn't always find me *perfectly* assertive!

Working with so many people over the years has given me enormous insight into different personalities, attitudes and approaches. I am grateful that so many people have opened up and shared a little bit of themselves for me to learn from.

# Introduction

As you read through this book it should become increasingly apparent that you are the main character of the plot. By the final chapter I hope you will understand and like that character more. If it has achieved its aim then this book will have helped you to:

- understand more about assertiveness and its importance as a life skill
- understand more about yourself and about why you behave in certain ways
- recognize the possibilities of changing and liberating the potential to be yourself
- use realistic tips for putting assertiveness into practice

In order to get the most from life, whatever our role, we have to work at sorting out relationships with other people. Using skills of assertiveness helps us to do that and this book will give you lots of ideas on how to become more effective in relating to others in both your personal life and your employment. However, the first relationship which we should address, and often the one we neglect, is with ourselves. The exercises and 'pauses for thought' in these chapters will give you the opportunity to spend some time constructively working on your relationship with yourself.

Whatever we do in our life, it is useful to have a tool kit to carry around which can help us deal with what comes along. In my kit, *assertiveness* is a major tool. In fact as I have learned more about being assertive it has become such a light device to carry that I am often not aware of it being there.

## Two cautionary notes before you go any further into these pages

The first is that it might seem that I am saying it is easy to be assertive. Well, often it isn't easy at all. The important thing is that *though it isn't easy it is worth it*. When you get it right it is a great feeling and it gives you confidence to tackle other issues. But, when it doesn't work, don't be too hard on yourself. Failing is bad enough without punishing yourself for it. Many people who are admired for their assertiveness confess to sometimes failing.

The second word of caution is not to take it all too seriously – this also implies not taking yourself too seriously. OK, we are looking at personal development and that rather old-fashioned notion of 'self-improvement', but it is essential to retain a sense of humour and perspective about the whole thing. We've all got hopes, fears, strengths, weaknesses, successes and failures, but we're only people.

# CHAPTER 1

# What does assertiveness really mean?

An interesting aspect of assertiveness is the response which the word itself evokes. Because much of my work involves me training, coaching and counselling people in assertiveness, it often comes up in general conversation. Some people are clear about what it means and have a personal view or tale to tell about their own experience of assertiveness. Then there are those who are worried they will look ignorant by asking what it actually means so they manoeuvre the conversation back to something more familiar.

The real gems come from people who *think*, mistakenly, that they understand what it is. Examples of responses I have received when I've told people that I run courses on assertiveness are:

- Cashier in a building society: '*oho! we'd like to be like that with our customers but unfortunately we have to be nice to them*'
- Receptionist in a dental surgery: '*you wouldn't get away with that here, we all have to get on with each other as a team*'
- Manager of a group of land surveyors: '*I don't go along with the idea of assertive management: I*

*handle my people with care, giving them the opportunity to do things their own way*'

- Person to whom I was introduced at a party: '*Yes, I can imagine that you are **very** assertive*' [meaning – I bet you are used to getting your own way you strident bitch!]

As you continue through this book I hope it will become clear to you how misguided these comments are – to the extent that you will be able to explain this kind of misconception next time you are confronted with it.

Becoming more assertive does not involve being unpleasant to people – getting away with behaviour which upsets a team or having a dictatorial management style. Neither are we talking about the aggressive individualism which was promoted in the 1980s.

**Being assertive is about respecting yourself enough to state what you want from other people. It is also about respecting other people and their right to express their own needs.**

Let's get it straight from the beginning: by using assertive behaviour you will not always get what you want or come out on top in a situation. People who criticize the notion of assertiveness, seeing it as behaviour which is pushy, demanding and self-important, don't understand its true meaning. Somewhere along the line it has become confused with aggression. What we are looking at in this book are clear distinctions of what assertiveness *really* is, how it *differs* from other behaviour styles and *why* it can be helpful in our lives.

Think now about somebody who you perceive as an assertive person – write down what they do which makes you see them that way. [In the light of what you have just read, are they assertive or were you like some of those people who had got the wrong impression?] Maybe they walk into a room *looking* comfortable and in control? Is it that they never appear to be flustered, apologetic or embarrassed if they make a mistake? Are they able to have straightforward relationships with many different people without getting trapped in webs of intrigue? Do they usually seem to know what they want?

Different people behave assertively in different ways. It is not a skill for cloning. The glory of human beings is that we are all so different. Our uniqueness is a treasure to be celebrated. We don't have to be assertive in the same way as somebody else. But we can be aware of our own self, informed about the concept of assertiveness and determined to live our life in a way that allows us to achieve our goals.

As you go through this book you will be invited to do some thinking about yourself and be offered suggestions on how behaving differently might be more effective for you. It is not, however, a step by step guide on how to run your life. Being yourself is the key to happiness and the more you understand about yourself, your behaviour and the behaviour of others, the more opportunity it gives you to be at your best.

**Assertiveness can be interpreted as:**
- behaviour
- self-confidence and self-esteem
- communication
- being able to fulfil our capabilities

**Assertiveness as Behaviour**
When we behave assertively we are in control – in control of ourselves, not controlling others. Let's face it, controlling one person is enough; no wonder we get

5

exhausted trying to manipulate control of other people as well.

Looking as though we are in control not only helps us to feel better but also influences other people. Imagine the person who comes into a meeting, papers hugged to their chest, head down, muttering a greeting. Do you think 'Aha! this person is going to have something interesting to say' or do you dismiss them without a thought. Maybe you've not come across anybody like this, but then again, perhaps you haven't noticed them!

On the other hand, somebody who enters the room full of their own self-importance, hustling people to make a start and obviously determined to put their own needs first is likely to turn people off for different reasons.

The person who walks in looking organized, making eye contact with a friendly smile and a greeting is going to have a far more favourable effect. We are likely to warm to them, not feel threatened and actually look forward to hearing what they have to say. Of the three, this is the person who is most likely to achieve their aims *assertively*.

**What about you? Which one of these approaches is nearest to describing you?**
*Write* YES, NO or SOMETIMES *in answer to the following*:

1. Do you make comfortable eye contact with people when you greet them?
2. If you join a group of people do you scan all of its members?
3. In general, do you stand with your head up, shoulders relaxed, arms and hands in an open posture?
4. Do you speak clearly and directly, keeping your

voice calm and controlled?
5. Do you show interest in other people by smiling and responding to them?

Ask people to help you answer the questions above – about their perception of you. Maybe you haven't been able to answer with a straight YES or NO, so think about specific situations.

- When do you appear confident and in control?
- When don't you?
- What would help you to transfer that comfort and confidence from one situation to another?

When we behave assertively we give the impression of being comfortable with ourselves and of being happy to occupy the space we stand in.

## ASSERTIVENESS FOR BUILDING SELF-CONFIDENCE AND SELF-ESTEEM

Think about a situation where you have been in a disagreement with somebody and you have failed to state your point of view. How do you feel afterwards? Angry? Put down? Do you replay the whole incident adding what you could, should or wish you'd have said and frequently chastise yourself for not saying these things? You may become more and more angry, but really the anger is not with the other person, it is with yourself – for not standing your ground, for not being quick witted, articulate or brave enough to counter the attack, however subtle, from the other person. '*Why did I let them speak to me like that*', '*Why didn't I just say . . .*', '*Who do they think they are . . .?*' The more we chew over this the more we eat into our self-esteem. We feel that we have let ourselves down, allowed someone to 'get the better of us'. The incident leaves an after-taste. On the other hand, when we find ourselves in a potentially difficult situation with somebody, and we handle it well, we walk away feeling good about ourselves. Which one of these feelings lasts longest? It is usually the negative feelings which hang around.

When we are assertive we feel good about ourselves because we let other people know how they can treat us. We don't feel intimidated by other people because we have a realistic, healthy measure of our own self-worth. Chapter 5 in this book will give you the opportunity to work on your own self-esteem and confidence but as a little taster, write down something about *you* which makes it worth spending time and effort developing your self-expression and views.

*I am worthwhile because* . . . . . . . . . . . . . . . . . . . . . .

## ASSERTIVENESS AS A WAY OF COMMUNICATING WITH PEOPLE

When we communicate assertively we say what we mean and mean what we say by giving clear, straightforward messages. You can read more about Positive Constructive Communication in Chapter 10. Here we look at the basic principles of communicating assertively.

### Be Direct
If there is something to be said then don't pussy-foot around, get on and say it. Avoid the tendency to use pre-ambles like: '*I know you're really busy but . . .*', '*I'm ever so sorry to trouble you . . .*', '*You'll probably think I'm*

*awful saying this . . .'*. These give the other person the opportunity to anticipate what we might be going to say and adopt a defensive or dismissive attitude. It is far more effective to directly state what we are trying to put across to somebody. That doesn't mean that we have to be rude, abrupt or unpleasant. It merely means that we give the impression of having considered what we want to communicate before we actually launch into sound. This gains respect from others as it prevents clouding the message.

### Be appropriate

Communication is most successful when the 'sender' is sensitive to the 'receiver'. I am not advocating that we should change our style of communicating to suit who we are with, but a degree of sensitivity to the other person will help. For example, if you are in the company of an elderly relative who expresses views about 'the youth of today' or the 'downfall of society' it might be appropriate to go along with them rather than express rational arguments to prove them wrong! If you are making a point to your boss then your style might be different from that of criticizing your partner. Not only the person, but the time and place should influence how appropriate it is to assert yourself. It might be more appropriate to let some things go. If you are choosing then this is not passive, but assertive.

### Taking responsibility

'I think . . .', 'In my opinion . . .', 'My understanding is . . .' are all far more effective ways of putting across our view than 'You are . . .', 'That's not right . . .'. And 'It isn't like that . . .'. We have the right to our opinions but ours is not the only opinion. People will be far more receptive to being told things about themselves if it is offered as your opinion rather than a universal statement. Think about the effect these statements have.

1. *'Your driving is terrible.'*
2. *'That outfit doesn't suit you.'*
3. *'You can't say that.'*
4. *'You never clean the bath out properly.'*
5. *'You were horrible to me last night.'*
6. *'That won't work, you should do it like this.'*

The responses are likely to be defensive or confrontational. Taking ownership of what you are saying will result in the other person being less threatened and more amenable to listening to you.

**Assertive alternatives:**
1. *'I think you drive too fast sometimes/I don't always feel very confident driving with you.'*
2. *'I'm not sure that I'm keen on that outfit on you.'*
3. *'I don't agree with what you are saying.'*
4. *'I would like to explain the way I like the bath to be cleaned.'*
5. *'I was upset about the way I felt you were treating me last night.'*
6. *'I would approach that differently, have you thought about doing it this way?'*

These approaches will not be seen as a put-down, nor as 'nagging' and because of that people will be more attuned to listen to your view.

**Remain calm and in control**
It is difficult to be assertive when your shoulders are hunched right up to your earlobes, your fists are clenched and your face is red. Taking deep breaths and letting some of the obvious tension drain from you will help. Being assertive spontaneously is more difficult than when we've had time to prepare what we want to say.

But a few seconds spent taking control of emotions will ensure that your brain is in gear before your tongue starts working. Of course, it's not only our words which communicate our message – body language speaks volumes. By controlling the tone and volume of your voice you can make the message less emotional. By ensuring that your body is relaxed and in tune with the words you are saying you become more plausible.

### Be willing to listen

The most overlooked aspect of communication is listening. People often think that good communication skills are about being articulate, telling a good tale, having a wide vocabulary. Yes, all of these are important, but the ability and willingness to listen to others is more important. We tend to fall into the category of either listening *distractedly* – allowing other things, whether in our head or around us to interfere; or *dismissively* – filtering only the bits which we want to take in. When we are listening to somebody we need to suspend judgement and emotion until we have heard them out and understood.

MUTUAL RESPECT is a vital aspect of assertiveness. Listening to the other person's point of view is as important as expressing our own view of a situation. 'But, that looks as if you are weak and going to give in to the other person,' some might say. This is not actually the case. When we are listening to somebody, as well as putting across our own view, we are actually more in control and therefore more assertive.

**Consider these questions about your own listening skills and tick the answer which is relevant to you.**

*Whilst the other person is talking, do you . . .*

|  | often | sometimes | never |
|---|---|---|---|
| Rehearse what you are going to say |  |  |  |
| Wish they would get to the point quickly |  |  |  |
| Interrupt |  |  |  |
| Mind-read |  |  |  |
| Judge them – by appearance or accent |  |  |  |
| Filter – what you already think/want to think |  |  |  |
| Daydream |  |  |  |

Most of us do some of these some of the time. We might think we are listening but we're not. When we communicate assertively we respect the other person's right to put their views across. They can't do this if we are not listening to them.

## ASSERTIVENESS FOR BEING YOURSELF

When we are assertive we state what we *think*, what we *feel* and what we *want*. In order to do this we have to put some thought into really understanding what it is we think, feel and want. This can mean that you have to let some things go – after all, with every gain there is loss. As you learn more about yourself and assertiveness, you will be able to weigh up what your profit and loss will be in handling situations more assertively. I hope you balance your books to achieve a huge net profit!

## CHAPTER 1 SUMMARY

- Assertiveness means standing up for your rights without violating the rights of others.
- Assertive behaviour appears comfortable, confident and in control.
- Assertiveness builds our self-esteem because we take care of our own needs.
- Assertive communication is direct, appropriate, responsible, calm and being willing to listen.
- Assertiveness allows you to understand yourself more and to be who you really are.

# CHAPTER 2

# Non-assertive behaviour and its results

Having looked at what assertive really is we are now going to consider behaviour which is *non-assertive*. In my experience most people who seek out assertiveness training and read books like these have a tendency to be passive and feel unhappy about not achieving what they want. Maybe they wish to be able to say 'no' to requests and stand up for themselves more. If this is you, then you will benefit tremendously from learning to become more assertive and putting it into practice. But, there is also a need for aggressive people to understand the consequences of their behaviour and recognize how it affects others.

What made you pick this book up? At this moment would you describe yourself as **assertive, aggressive** or **passive**? Have a look at the grid overleaf to clarify some of the basic elements of each type of behaviour.

With which of these boxes do you identify yourself.

It is unlikely that you will fit into one overall behaviour type completely but I'm sure you recognize that life is most comfortable straight down the middle of this grid. Not only in terms of behaving that way yourself, but being around other people who are like this.

You might also like to give some thought to some-

| WHEN WE BEHAVE PASSIVELY: | WHEN WE BEHAVE ASSERTIVELY: | WHEN WE BEHAVE AGGRESSIVELY: |
|---|---|---|
| WE ARE LIKELY TO BE TAKEN ADVANTAGE OF. | WE STAND UP FOR OUR RIGHTS AND RESPECT OTHER PEOPLE'S RIGHTS. | WE TAKE ADVANTAGE OF OTHERS. |
| WE FEEL FRUSTRATED, HURT, ANXIOUS AND RESENTFUL. | OUR SELF-ESTEEM IS GOOD. WE FEEL AND DISPLAY APPROPRIATE SELF-CONFIDENCE. | WE ARE DEFENSIVE. WE USE PUT-DOWNS AND BULLY TACTICS TO HUMILIATE OTHERS. |
| WE ARE WITHDRAWN AND INHIBITED. WE FEEL SOCIALLY INFERIOR. | WE EXPRESS OUR FEELINGS AND ARE COMFORTABLE IN SOCIAL SETTINGS. | WE SHOW ANGER AND HOSTILITY AND ARE UNPREDICTABLE IN SOCIAL SETTINGS. |
| WE LEAVE OTHER PEOPLE TO MAKE CHOICES FOR US. | WE CHOOSE FOR OURSELVES. | WE IMPINGE ON OTHER PEOPLE'S CHOICES. |
| WE DO NOT ACHIEVE OUR GOALS. | WE ACHIEVE GOALS FOR OURSELVES WITHOUT HURTING OTHER PEOPLE. | WE HAVE NO RESPECT FOR OTHERS' NEEDS AND ACHIEVE OUR GOALS REGARDLESS OF THEIRS. |

body else who has influence in your life – partner/boss/parent/friend/colleague. With which boxes would you identify them?

### An example: the car park

Imagine somebody knocks on your car window just as you are parking in a busy town centre. You have not been aware that the other person was trying to park in the same place, your mind is on getting to the bank before it shuts. They explain that they had been queuing for that parking space. Would you:

- Apologize profusely, feeling unnerved and anxious about the situation and move your car without question?

*or*

- Respond in a sarcastic or confrontational tone, claim your right to the territory, dismiss them and go about your business feeling like a winner?

Neither of these approaches would be assertive in their initial responses. The first suggests that you are willing to automatically subordinate your needs to the other person, the second implies that you have little or no regard for the other person's rights. The assertive approach would be to apologize calmly, explain that you hadn't been aware that they were waiting and negotiate to keep the parking space. I agree that this is an ideal response and that it is probably full of the 'old-world courtesy' that modern life doesn't always allow time for. But try to relate this to a situation where there is need for an ongoing relationship with the other person. If you constantly give in to their needs you are likely to feel frustrated and unhappy with yourself. How often do you walk or drive away from a situation thinking 'Why did I let them get away with that?' and 'Why didn't I say this?'

On the other hand, if your response to the parking situation is an aggressive one, is that also how you respond in other situations?

If so, what is it costing you in terms of your relationships with other people?

Do they anticipate aggression from you and therefore 'play safe' by not getting too close to the danger?

# LIKELY CONSEQUENCES OF
# NON-ASSERTIVE BEHAVIOUR

**When you behave passively:**

- Initially there can be a short-term reward –
  *you are perceived as 'nice' 'kind' 'helpful' 'gentle'.*
- But when you have said YES or gone along with something against your real will –
  *you feel regret and lose confidence.*
- This is usually reinforced when you want to make a request to somebody –
  *you feel uncomfortable stating your own needs.*

**This is likely to lead to a reduction in self-esteem and in personal effectiveness.**

- The original short-term reward is now lost and we experience reduced esteem from others –
  *people start to feel sorry for you, become irritated, and lose respect for you.*

**We are left with submerged anger, hurt, frustration which can lead to stress, broken relationships, unhappiness and depression.** Ironically people often behave passively in order to 'keep the peace' or 'anything for a quiet life'.

**When you behave aggressively:**

- There is a short-term reward –
  *you get it off your chest, you get noticed and some-times you are congratulated.*
- A state of conflict is established –
  *people fear or avoid you, they withdraw co-operation and build defences to ward off humiliation.*

This is likely to lead to isolation and a need for self-justification which reinforces the aggression. The personal result is a need to watch your back which causes loneliness and insularity. In the workplace, the organizational result is that energy and creativity are spent maintaining the state of conflict rather than channelled into making the business successful.

### Beware the wolf in sheep's clothing

So far we have been talking about two aspects of non-assertive behaviour which are fairly easy to recognize, passivity and aggression. Like most things in life, it isn't always so straightforward. Aggression is not always open and obvious, it can be hidden cleverly with the result that it is more pernicious than the loud, shouting style of aggression. Similarly, the most seemingly passive people can actually be very manipulative in spreading feelings of guilt and responsibility amongst others.

## DISGUISED AGGRESSION

If you have watched the classic television series *Fawlty Towers* then you may recognize the sarcastic humour used by Basil Fawlty as a put-down to the receiver. The roll of the eyes, the 'clever' jokes are invariably at the other person's expense. Maybe you can remember situations from your school-days when a teacher humiliated you by cleverly showing you up in front of the class. Sarcasm, although often very amusing to observe, can be extremely painful when you are on the receiving end. It can result in people avoiding too much involvement with the sarcastic person for fear of feeling or looking stupid.

Another example of disguised aggression is being

*two-faced* – saying something about a person but never telling that person what you really think. This actually denies the individual the opportunity of explaining themselves or changing their behaviour to something which would be more acceptable. Huddling together to share gossip about a person can feel like fun but if you need to have a relationship with that person, for whatever reason, it can be hard to meet their eye. An assertive person will refuse to get drawn into gossip about people – if there is something to be said they will talk *directly* to the person (using the techniques outlined in Chapter 1).

## MANIPULATIVE BEHAVIOUR

Somebody who sits in a meeting saying nothing, might appear to be passive, but if they leave the meeting determined to sabotage a decision then beware the sting in the tail. Somebody who constantly bemoans their inability to get what they want from people but when asked, are unable to express their desires, can instil an enormous amount of confusion and guilt in others.

By not asserting real feelings, manipulative behaviour allows people to maintain and fuel their own dissatisfaction whilst ensuring that other people don't have a good time either! The tool they are using is guilt. This can be seen in family relationships where the 'martyr' mother is continually doing 'everything for everybody' and asking nothing for herself. It is natural that if we constantly give, without receiving, then we will start to feel resentful and hurt. Imagine that you have a full jug of water at the beginning of the day and as you go through the day you keep pouring it out for people. If the jug is not frequently topped up, what remains isn't very generous. If we don't top up our emotional jug, if we don't take care of our own needs, what we are giving can become pretty frugal. The resentment we feel is often turned on other people either through open aggression or a manipulative, disguised aggression whose aim is to arouse guilt and discomfort. WE and only WE can be responsible for our feelings and the recognition and expression of our needs, in order that other people can choose whether or not to meet them.

Chapter 4 will give you the opportunity to look at some choices which are open to you. Whilst there are various reasons – upbringing, cultural influence, personality – which influence the way we instinctively behave, we *are* capable of taking a step back and choosing our behaviour, rather than being locked into one pattern of responses.

**When we are assertive we teach people how we would like them to behave towards us.**

## CHAPTER 2 SUMMARY

- When people behave AGGRESSIVELY they are only concerned with meeting their own needs.
- When people behave PASSIVELY they subordinate their own needs in order to please others.
- When people behave MANIPULATIVELY they blame others for their own frustration or unhappiness.
- When people behave ASSERTIVELY they demonstrate that they respect their own rights and that they respect those of others.

# CHAPTER 3

# What's in it for you?

By now you will have probably developed a good under-standing of the different types of behaviour. Maybe you have recognized yourself in some of the descriptions. OK, so what if you have? First of all, it will be counter-productive if you are starting to reprimand yourself for it! Remember, self-development is concerned with rec-ognizing strengths and weaknesses – capitalizing on the strengths and working towards eliminating the weak-nesses.

## PUTTING SOME ASSERTIVE BEHAVIOUR
## INTO PRACTICE

Somebody for whom I have a great deal of respect and admiration confided to me that he had been through a period when he lacked confidence and behaved non-assertively during a time of business failure and un-employment. He talked of building a protective wall of passivity around himself which prevented him from taking risks and therefore becoming more hurt. His view was that people reading a book on assertiveness might expect that they will be given a manageable challenge to go out and try. Below, I have described one activity which he found helpful – I invite you to see if it helps you.

Visit a car boot sale to barter for small items. If you fail at the first stall then try the next and with a bit of luck, by the end of the market, you will have achieved success and an armful of items you don't need. But most importantly, you will have practised responding to 'competition' with strangers, knowing it will not have any dire consequences.

Exercise:
*From the list below, put a tick against those situations which you feel that you do handle assertively, which means you will:*

- Leave the situation feeling OK about yourself and OK about the other person involved
- There will be a WIN/WIN outcome in terms of mutual respect and self-respect
- There will be an absence of anxiety afterwards – you won't have feelings of guilt, embarrassment or frustration

## Group A
1. Sending food back in a restaurant.
2. Asking somebody to return something they have borrowed.
3. Expressing your opinions in a meeting.
4. Asking somebody to do you a favour.
5. Confronting a neighbour about something you are not happy with.
6. Negotiating over your salary or something you want to sell.
7. Trying to get somebody in authority to listen to your viewpoint.

8. Questioning a doctor or hospital consultant.
9. Making conversation with strangers in a social situation.

**Group B**
1. Dealing with doorstep/telephone sales people.
2. Accepting criticism.
3. Conflict at home or at work.
4. Losing an argument.
5. Saying 'No' to somebody in authority.
6. Saying 'No' to somebody in your family.
7. Accepting a compliment.
8. Declining a social invitation.
9. Unsolicited sexual advances.

Having ticked the ones which you feel you *do* handle assertively, which group scores the most ticks?

Group A deals with SENDER skills, i.e. those initiated by you, whereas Group B are RECEIVER skills which require an assertive response to another person's behaviour, regardless of whether that behaviour has been assertive, aggressive or passive. Receiver skills are the more difficult and often are dealt with instinctively rather than thoughtfully.

Take a look at some possible responses to these situations and try to identify whether in each case the example represents ASSERTIVE, AGGRESSIVE or PASSIVE behaviour.

**1. Sending food back in a restuarant**
a. *'Excuse me. What do you call this offering? These vegetables are disgusting. You've no right serving food like this.'*
b. *'Excuse me, I think these vegetables have been heated up from lunchtime. They don't taste very*

    *nice. Would you please take them away and see what*
    *else you can offer me.'*

c. *Saying nothing, not enjoying the meal and then feel-*
    *ing aggrieved because you have wasted money.*

'a' is an AGGRESSIVE response because it is a put-down. It is a personal attack tinged with sarcasm and arrogance. [A very cautionary note here – I once worked in a wine bar with a lively young woman called Linda. Her response to this person would have been a blood-chilling grin; she would then spit on the new vegetables before taking them out with a flourish. There are some things in life that it's better not to know!]

    'b' is an ASSERTIVE response. It is reasonable objective and polite.

    'c' is a PASSIVE response because the person is likely to feel disappointed and may be angry that they didn't say anything. They are also likely to have bad feelings about the eating place without giving the staff the opportunity to put things right. There might be times when not saying anything is your choice, maybe because you are in a hurry, or it would detract from the occasion. In this case it is assertive to choose *not* to take action, as long as you don't proceed to moan about it, or feel cross with yourself afterwards.

    Which of these would be your normal response?

    What will you do next time you are in a situation similar to this?

## 2. Asking somebody to return something they have borrowed

a. *'I'm ever so sorry, I know it's really rude of me to ask*
    *this. But you know that book which I lent you a few*
    *months ago? Well, one of my friends said he'd like to*

read it so do you think you could let me have it back when you've finished with it?'

b. 'You've still got that book I let you borrow in the summer. I want it now and I'm never lending you anything again.'

c. 'I lent you a book called **Perfect Assertiveness** some time ago, I'd like it back please. Could you bring it into work on Monday?'

'a' is PASSIVE because you haven't given a clear message that you definitely want it back.

'b' is AGGRESSIVE because it is an over-reaction which is likely either to make the other person feel bad, or evoke an argument.

'c' is ASSERTIVE because you have stated what you want and given the person the opportunity to say whether or not they can deliver.

Which of these would be your normal response?

What will you do next time you are in a situation similar to this?

## 3. Dealing with doorstep or telephone sales people

a. 'I'm afraid my husband isn't here at the moment.' [persistent response from sales person] 'Well perhaps you would like to call back later, although I don't really think we are interested.'

b. 'Thank you for the call. We are really not interested in buying anything from you. There is no point in either of us wasting time. All the best, goodbye.'

c. 'What do you think this is, knocking on my door like this. You can stuff your double glazing right up!?~# Clear off you!?~#.'

'a' is a PASSIVE response and will only serve to prolong the time-wasting.

'b' is ASSERTIVE and acknowledges that the sales-person has a job to do but that you are not a potential customer. There is no personal attack.

'c' is AGGRESSIVE – and you will not be surprised to hear – is the most common response. Fair enough; it can be obtrusive to have people disturbing you and try-ing to sell you something you haven't expressed interest in. But, after all, like most of us, they are only trying to make a living. The law allows people to knock on your door, it is not their personal vendetta against you. As individuals, they do have the right to be treated with respect. This scenario is often used as an opportunity by people who are frustrated with their passive behaviour in important situations. They see it as sport to try and humiliate sales people. Maybe it is something to do with an Englishman's home being his castle. Well, if that's what you want, build a moat.

Which of these would be your normal response?

What will you do next time you are in a situation similar to this?

## 4. Declining a social invitation

a. '*Oh, thanks very much. I'd really love to come but I'm ever so busy this week. I'm really sorry. I would have come but I've got to take the dog to the vet, clean out the garage, write a letter to my aunt in Montreal, give a . . .*'
b. '*You're always asking me to go there with you. Can't you find some other mug?*'
c. '*Thanks for asking, but that's really not my kind of evening. Enjoy it anyway.*'

'a' is PASSIVE because it smacks of excuses. It is also extremely self-centred as the only information the other person really needs is 'are you going, or not?'

'b' is AGGRESSIVE – once again it is a put-down.

'c' is an ASSERTIVE message which leaves the other person clear about how you feel.

Which of these would be your normal response?

What will you do next time you are in a situation similar to this?

## 5. Accepting Criticism

a. '*What do you mean by that? I did a perfectly good job, you're not so great at doing that yourself.*'
b. '*I'm sorry. I'll do it again. Didn't mean to upset you.*'
c. '*It would be useful if you could go through it with me and tell me exactly what it is you think is wrong with what I did.*'

'a' is AGGRESSIVE in that it is defensive and attacking at the same time. The person is unlikely to learn anything from this response as they are denying the other person the opportunity to be more specific about their criticism.

'b' is PASSIVE because they are immediately taking the blame on board and bringing emotion into the situation.

'c' is ASSERTIVE and should result in the person getting more information about what they are being criticized for. If the criticism is valid then it becomes a learning opportunity; if not, then it can lead to objective further discussion.

Which of these would be your normal response?

What will you do next time you are in a situation similar to this?

[In Chapter 9 we will look closely at the thorny issue of saying 'NO'.]

*Now go back to the lists you ticked earlier. For each of the situations which you felt you didn't handle assertively write your* **normal** *response and then write down what your* **assertive** *response would be.*

**No. 1 Situation:**
My normal response . . .

How I will respond assertively . . .

**No. 2 Situation:**
My normal response . . .

How I will respond assertively . . .

**No. 3 Situation:**
My normal response . . .

How I will respond assertively . . .

**No. 4 Situation:**
My normal response . . .

How I will respond assertively . . .

**No. 5 Situation:**
My normal response . . .

How I will respond assertively . . .

**No. 6 Situation:**
My normal response . . .

How I will respond assertively . . .

I know this is hard work. It involves some fairly deep thinking and a few self discoveries which may be painful. We've learned that there is no such thing as a free lunch and I add to that there is no such thing as pain-free personal development. If we are going to achieve change we must be able to see the benefits of our hard work. In order to remind yourself what you will get out of your investment, give some thought to these four questions:

- What do I get out of behaving passively?
- What do I get out of behaving aggressively?
- What will I have to give up in order to become more assertive?
- What will I gain from being more assertive?

## CHAPTER 3 SUMMARY

- When you have handled a situation assertively you feel OK about yourself and the other person.
- When you have been assertive there is an absence of anxiety – you don't feel guilty, embarrassed or frustrated.
- Knowing what the benefits are will help you to be more determined to be assertive.

## CHAPTER 4

# You're in charge

## FIGHT, FLIGHT, OR SOMEWHERE OVER THE RAINBOW!

When we were animals in the jungle we were equipped with the wonderful capacity to respond to danger with either a fight or flight response. *Fight* can represent aggressive behaviour, whilst *flight* may be a passive response. When we do respond instinctively in either of these ways it usually results in us having regrets later. The car park scenario in Chapter 2 identifies these two positions – the passive *flight* or the aggressive *fight* each represent spontaneous responses which are not assertive. There is a whole spectrum of behaviour to choose from which we often fail to draw upon.

How often do you spend the day in the passive end of this arc – taking flight from difficult situations and avoiding saying what you really think?

– '*Yes, of course I'll do that for you.*'
– '*No, sure, it's all right, I can stay late.*'

Then you get home, kick the cat, bang the cupboards, yell at the kids . . . suddenly you are in fight mode – all because you took the 'easy' option.

The arc diagram represents the choices open to us.

30

## The behaviour rainbow

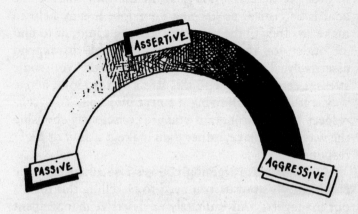

*Ian Yates*

Sometimes it might be appropriate to be passive – with certain people, on certain days, in certain situations. As we said earlier, if an elderly relative is chuntering on about 'the youth of today' or making other sweeping statements with which you strongly disagree, it might be easier, for the sake of the situation and others involved, to bite your tongue, smile and nod and take the completely passive stance.

### Behaviour in the workplace
In the increasingly competitive world of work it might not be expedient for you to behave assertively with some people who are in authority over you. I say this regretfully, but with a realistic awareness that not all managers and people in authority are assertive and that a certain amount of 'game-playing' is necessary for survival in some organizations. To maintain your self-

esteem when forced into such a situation it is essential that you are aware that you are *choosing* this behaviour in order to achieve your goals at the time; maybe the goal is as critical as keeping your job. It may help to make an effigy of the person to stick pins into, or to find an outlet for the energy you are unable to expend assertively. The situation is likely to cause you some stress. Learn to deal with this stress in a positive, active way, rather than allowing it to eat into you. Your self-respect will be stronger if you are consciously choosing the way you behave, rather than making a *fight* or *flight* response.

On workplace training courses I so often hear the comment, 'It's not us you need to be telling this to; it's our managers.' Unfortunately an assertive management style is not as common as people might think. Managers may have a reputation for being assertive, but as people learn about what assertiveness *really* is, a realization dawns that the style of management they are used to is actually aggressive.

Organizations no longer have rigid hierarchical structures with armies of people to do the work. When they did, it was fairly effective to pay a workforce to do as they were told and managers to tell them. In today's competitive world of work employers need people to use initiative, to be committed to quality and prepared to take ownership of problems. This is best achieved by behaving assertively towards employees and encouraging them to be assertive. There is often an underlying ethos of fear which is partly due to job insecurity. As a result of this fear an aggressive, back-stabbing environment can grow in which blame consumes more energy than shared problem-solving. Fear might be a good short-term motivator, but eventually it destroys creativity and promotes conflict rather than co-operation.

Chapter 11 will teach you more about how to maintain assertive discipline at work.

If you are working in this type of environment then you are probably experiencing pressure and stress. We all respond in different ways to pressure – many of us thrive on it. It is important that you understand how stress affects you in order to minimize the potential damage these negative aspects of stress can cause to your health and general well-being.

**Acting on stress**
It is essential for a healthy life that we **ACT** on stress.

**A for Awareness**
**C for Confrontation**
**T for Therapy**

**Awareness** means learning about what stress actually is, how it affects you as an individual and how it might be affecting people around you.

**Confrontation** of those who cause your stress. Doing something about them in order to be more in control. This usually involves time management, organization and assertiveness.

**Therapy** is treating yourself well. It doesn't have to mean lying on a couch paying somebody to listen to you, although if that is helpful, then why not. But it is more about remembering that you have needs – remembering the person you are when you are *not* under stress and living in the present and experiencing the moment rather than always having one foot on the way to where you've got to go next.

Take control of your life. A balanced life will always have ups and downs – feeling those ups and downs, knowing when they are happening to you and choosing the best way to deal with them promotes a well-being from which we are able to be assertive.

## When aggression is the necessary choice

There may be times when choosing to be aggressive will be the most effective or appropriate behaviour. If somebody is being very unpleasant and you want to get rid of them, it may be better to be slightly aggressive. Some situations of sexual behaviour could be avoided if people gave clearer messages about what is unacceptable to them, rather than worrying about offending the other person or looking stupid. The main purpose is to get your point across and if somebody is behaving in an aggressive way with you it might be more appropriate to behave aggressively back. **You are in charge. You can choose.** We don't have to behave in a certain way because 'that's the way we are'. We can decide which is the best way to behave in order to achieve our objective in each specific situation.

In Chapter 3 we saw that it is often easier and more effective to plan assertiveness, as spontaneous reactions are more likely to become *fight* or *flight* responses. Sometimes though, we indulge in a more negative form of stalling. Allow me to introduce you to a new slant on the hobby of stamp collecting.

## Stamp Collecting

The phrase *stamp collecting* offers a graphic explanation of how people save up all their angst and then POW! – they let somebody have it. Maybe you have been on the receiving end of this? Let's see if it rings any bells with you.

Do you remember Green Shield stamps? They were given away with petrol and various products before technology turned everything into a credit card look-alike. Once you'd collected several thousand of them, they could be cashed in for a thermos flask or something similar which was probably not relevant to your needs at the time.

Well, think about yourself as you go through the day, the week, the years – somebody says or does something to you which you don't like. Rather than responding assertively, you store it up, in other words, you lick a stamp and stick it in your memory 'book'. The same person or somebody else says or does something, and this is another stamp . . . and so it goes on. After a while you've got a really big collection and every now and then it can be taken out and inspected to assess the hurt, humiliation and frustration other people have caused you – the unfairness of life. Then one day, something snaps and causes you to cash in *all* of your stamps. You really let somebody have it. It probably isn't one of the people who gave you loads to collect – the amount you cash in with that person is probably disproportionate to their actual contribution to your collection, but nevertheless, they are getting it anyway! Familiar?

Can you think of a situation when you have been on the receiving end of this?

Can you remember the person's body language and tone of voice?

It is likely that at the time they were trying to hurt, humiliate and blame you for their own feelings, whilst justifying their own righteousness. This kind of behaviour can be seen in all kinds of scenarios.

### Example
Susan, a mother at home, feels that she is constantly giving to everybody around her and, consequently, has a lot of unexpressed feelings about her situation – it might be resentment, disappointment, frustration, whatever. She submerges the feelings – *stamp-collects* them – and then

cashes them in over something fairly trivial like a broken glass, muddy feet or a borrowed pair of tights. The receiver of the stamps will be mystified at the outburst over something seemingly trivial and will probably dismiss it as 'nagging'.

## Example

Keith is a supervisor in a shop where the staff enjoy a relaxed, sociable working environment but are rather sloppy in terms of customer attitudes and tidiness. He is aware that staff take advantage of his passive style and one day he criticizes a till mistake, issuing stern, non-specific, indiscriminate disciplinary warnings out of the blue. The people receiving these stamps will not know what is actually expected of them. It is unlikely they will retain any respect for the supervisor or be prepared to change their work habits.

Having allowed themselves to be at the left-hand side of the rainbow arc (flight) in certain situations, Susan and Keith have now swung to the other side (fight) and expended the energy which they've been holding in check. If Susan points out to her family just what it is she feels she gives to them and tells them what she would like in return, then a dialogue will have begun which can take them forward and bypass barriers of resentment. Keith needs to tell his staff the standards which are expected of them and ensure that he gives constructive feedback, rather than *stamp collecting* when standards are not maintained.

By storing up hurt and humiliation we can build a 'case' for ourselves and justify negative feelings about other people. We may have been taught that anger is unacceptable and learned to shy away from conflict. The act of cashing in our collection of stamps will probably mean displacing the anger – towards the wrong person, in the wrong situation, with a disproportionate response to one particular incident. As we said earlier, there might be a short-term reward to this in terms of 'getting it off your chest' but the longer-term consequences are likely to be uncomfortable, either in your feelings about yourself, or your relationship with the other person. That other person becomes a scapegoat.

Are you sitting comfortably? Then maybe this is an opportunity for you to take out your stamp collection. Write down situations or relationships where you can recognize that you have *stamp-collected*.

What can you do in order to deal assertively with some of the hurt or resentment you might have put down on paper? Having identified these, perhaps by the time you get to the end of this book, you will feel ready to start tackling them. On the other hand, maybe some of them are out of date and irrelevant to your life as it is right now. It might be better for you to let some of these go. Yes, you may have been aggrieved, but nobody ever said life would be fair. Stamp collecting involves time and emotional energy. You have to find somewhere to store the stamps and whenever you come across them you have to indulge in a bit of self-pity. Have you really got so much spare time in your life that you can afford to do this? *Never forget that in life there is no dress rehearsal.*

Don't collect stamps. Like Green Shield stamps they are things of the past. Learn to choose appropriate behaviour at the time so that you are not swinging like a pendulum across the behaviour arc.

**Other people are not responsible for our behaviour or our feelings – we are. Assertiveness is about taking responsibility for ourselves, not blaming other people for our own unhappiness.**

If somebody hurts you then you have every right to

feel the pain of that hurt, but hanging on to it and allowing it to contaminate your general well-being is a waste of your life. Others can only affect us in so much as we allow them to. Who is in charge of your life? Are your arms raised and your hands free in order to be the conductor of your life, or are they being manipulated like a marionette having its strings pulled?

**You are in charge. You control your feelings. You can make choices about how you respond and behave.**

## CHAPTER 4 SUMMARY

- Visualize behaviour as an arc from which you can choose responses.
- There are situations when assertiveness might not be the most appropriate behaviour.
- Dealing with things at the time, rather than storing them up – *stamp collecting* – is more healthy and releases emotional energy for positive living.

# CHAPTER 5

# Learn to be your own best friend

If you are thinking that learning to become more assertive is not easy then I agree with you. This book may read as though I am saying it's a piece of cake. Ducking out of tricky situations by being passive, or striking out aggressively when your back is to the wall, is behaviour which comes all too easily. Ask my kids, ask my husband, ask my colleagues, ask my friends and ask the guys from the Gas Board who demolished my heating system!

What I am certain of, though, is that however difficult assertiveness is, it is worth the effort. It can lead to a happier, calmer, more fulfilling and joyous existence for the individual and for the people around them. Nobody really likes a wimp, least of all the person who is one! Nobody wants to get close to an aggressor – you wouldn't put your hand into a tiger's cage, would you?

## KNOWING YOUR RIGHTS

A basic concept of assertiveness is the notion of people having rights. Being confident of what those rights are, enables us to behave in a way which leads to greater fulfilment and personal satisfaction. However, it is not only our rights, but also the rights of others which need to be considered.

I was recently working with an organization in a consultancy role, with the objective of improving the service they gave to their customers. Once I started to understand the company, it became clear – not unusually – that there was a great deal of internal conflict going on between departments and individuals. My view is that the service received by customers is usually a reflection of what goes on internally; clearly, in this case there was a need for increased co-operation and relationship building. The staff were in agreement with this, so when my colleague and I presented to the board what we intended to do, we put forward the notion of an internal Bill of Rights. Whoops! How much we learn from our mistakes! The Managing Director declared the whole idea as unpalatable – he viewed it as subversive and launched into a tirade of 'the trouble with this country . . . rights . . . too many rights . . .' The upshot was that he didn't really listen to the rest of our presentation and we had to work hard to rebuild credibility.

Maybe you too had a similar response when I introduced the word rights. If so, please don't throw the book across the room! When we talk about rights in assertiveness there is a recognition that they are everybody's rights, therefore, we also have the *responsibility* to respect the rights of others. To give you an example I would like to present to you what I acknowledge as a BILL OF RIGHTS.

**I BELIEVE I HAVE THE RIGHT TO:**
1. ASK FOR WHAT I WANT. This doesn't mean I will always get it!
2. EXPRESS MY OPINIONS AND MY FEELINGS

AND SHOW EMOTION. Doing this in an *assertive* way will mean doing it in a way appropriate to the situation.

3. NOT BE DISCRIMINATED AGAINST. To be judged on my merit, not my age, sex, race etc . . .

4. MAKE MY OWN DECISIONS AND COPE WITH THE CONSEQUENCES. Resist being influenced by what others say I 'should' do.

5. CHOOSE WHETHER OR NOT TO GET INVOLVED WITH SOMEONE ELSE'S PROBLEMS. A 'caring' person doesn't have to be all things to all people. Sometimes it is necessary to distinguish between having a responsibility **towards** others and being responsible **for** others.

6. MAKE MISTAKES. Learn from them and improve, but not store up guilt over my errors.

7. GET WHAT I PAY FOR. Whether buying something, employing somebody or using a service.

8. CHANGE MY MIND. As we personally develop our outlook expands; we don't have to hold on to the same views. If I listen to somebody else assertively, I might realize they are right and I was wrong.

9. PRIVACY. Of thought, space, personal issues.

10. BE SUCCESSFUL. In our society there is a tendency to play down, almost apologize for our achievements and joys. It is OK to celebrate them.

Feeling I have 'Rights' helps my self-respect and enhances my confidence to 'go for it'. Equally it is important to acknowledge that other people share those rights and therefore are entitled to be respected for them.

You may disagree with some of these, or wish to add your own. An interesting and worthwhile application of drawing up a Bill of Rights is to do it as a family, as colleagues or as a group of people coming together for whatever reason.

**Family Bill of Rights**
Home life can bring all sorts of tensions; some people may feel they are being taken for granted, others may feel that there are too many restrictions – all sorts of dynamics are going on and often we don't address them. Whilst parents have responsibility to their children they also have the right to some privacy and personal space. Children need discipline and structure, but they also have the right to explanations of why certain behaviour is or is not acceptable. The process of talking about one another's rights and drawing up a bill or charter will be very illuminating in terms of understanding how each member of the family perceives their own world within that family.

**A team charter**
A group of people working together can remove some of the barriers and blocks to effective communication by participating in a discussion based around the notion of 'what is and what isn't OK in this team'. I recently facil-itated this with a group of busy people working in an open-plan office; they designed their 'bill'. All sorts of things came out about social chit-chat and disruptive behaviour which clearly had needed saying for some time. The outcome was that people felt more able to ask for quiet, or to move away from time-wasters without it causing conflict or offence.

As with many problem-solving exercises, the *process* of discussing issues is as valuable as the *content* of the final Bill of Rights. It will not work well if people are defensive. They need to be open to receive and offer crit-icism in a constructive, assertive way (using the guide to assertive communication outlined in Chapter 1). People have, on many occasions, found this notion of rights liberating. It has helped them to move forward positively and see assertiveness as their tool for becoming more fulfilled.

## YOU HAVE THE RIGHT TO BE ASSERTIVE

Self-esteem is both a cause and an effect of assertiveness. We can have such a good time learning to work on our weaknesses and celebrate our strengths – if only we will let ourselves.

**Exercise**
*What I would like you to do now is take a pen and complete the lines below with a positive statement about your strengths. Try to focus on qualities rather than skills. Make sure that what you write is positive.*

*Try to go for qualities – e.g. I am happy/I am generous/I am loving/I am honest with myself/I am good fun (rather than I am a good driver/cook/parent/ golfer etc.)*

I am . . .

I am . . .

I am . . .

I am . . .

I am . . .

*Don't stop here, if you can think of more please go on writing them down.*

Sometimes on Assertiveness Training Courses this task is met with excruciating embarrassment both from men and women. There is a lot of wriggling, pen-chewing, crossing out, head shaking. Of course, there are usually a few people who do it immediately and with obvious pleasure. A group of Americans are likely to say 'Gee, only five?' but that is the exception.

If you are struggling with this, what would your best friend or somebody close to you write about you? What are the qualities that attract them to you? Not what you do for them, but the essential **you**, the person you are when you are relaxed, happy and at your best?

When you have completed this task, read through your list of 'I Am's', take in a deep breath and appreciate yourself and your right to be assertive.

**Learn to carve your strengths in marble and write your weaknesses in sand.**

## CHAPTER 5 SUMMARY

- We all have rights – the process of stating what they are can bring us closer to understanding each other and respecting one another's needs.
- A personal Bill of Rights is self-affirming and increases our confidence to be assertive.
- Respecting our own and other people's rights is the root of assertive behaviour.
- Be your own best friend, be kind to yourself and *like* yourself.
- You have the right to be assertive because you are worth it.

# CHAPTER 6

# Moving on, letting go

I am often asked whether some people are 'naturally' more assertive than others and whether I believe that assertiveness is instinctive in some people. This is the 'big one' – the debate about nature versus nurture in personality and behaviour. Have we inherited our characteristics or are we the product of our environment?

My personal view is that we are a mixture of both of these fundamental influences. All of us have inherited characteristics and traits which form part of our genetic make up; all of us have had experiences which have influenced our personality and behaviour. Some of us have been luckier than others, but above all, we are all equipped with the capacity for change. We are not fixed into certain patterns of thought or behaviour. If we believe too rigidly that the influence of *either* nature or nurture has set our behavioural destiny, then that belief can become an explanation and an excuse for why we can't change and do things differently.

Some people retreat from taking positive steps which would improve their life. They build a protective comfort zone around themselves from which they inhabit life. Stepping out of that comfort zone is very difficult, even though life within the zone is not necessarily truly comfortable. When people are in counselling or a process of self-development, they sometimes come up against a realization which highlights a need for changing their behaviour or attitude. Although they can see that the change would bring real benefits to them, it becomes clear that this change is too difficult for them to undertake. This can often be observed in a physical withdrawal – they might fold their arms tightly across their chest saying 'well, this is me; this is the way I am'. Or there is a long 'Mmm . . .' and a nod of the head, usually signifying that they have arrived at this water's edge before but it is always too difficult to take the plunge so they are going to retreat once again. Perhaps you can relate to this by looking back on a number of New Year's resolutions you have made and broken over the years. Knowing what needs to change is not the same as making it happen.

**Is assertiveness instinctive in some of us? Is it *natural* behaviour?**

What is your view? I am certain that it comes more naturally to some than others. I think that once we are aware of what it can do for us and we use it consciously it becomes internalized as part of our habitual behaviour.

Young children can be instinctively assertive. Ask a child of two or three years of age if they want to go for a walk and they will answer 'Yes' or 'No' spontaneously. Ask an adult and they will probably say 'Well, what would you like to do?' Through the process of conditioning, children learn that passive behaviour is seen as more acceptable to those around them – in order to gain approval they adapt, losing their natural capacity for assertiveness. Young children also have a natural capacity for aggression, but once they begin to learn that this is seen as unacceptable to people around them, they disguise or subdue their natural capacity for aggressiveness, sometimes replacing this with other styles of nonassertive behaviour such as manipulation or disguised aggression.

## PARENT-ADULT-CHILD

A theory which I find very useful in helping me to gain a better understanding of people is that of Transactional Analysis or TA; which was first developed by Eric Berne, an American psychiatrist and psychotherapist. He observed certain patterns of thought and behaviour in his patients and developed his observations into a psychological model which can be very easily explained.

Basically, the theory suggests that each of us has three *ego states* from which we operate, regardless of our age or status; these are *parent-adult-child* and are always represented like this:

Our *PARENT* is a mixture of the rules and norms which were passed to us in the early stages of development – the **taught** element.

Our *CHILD* represents how we received the messages which were going on around us, the feelings which they evoked – the **felt** element.

Our *ADULT* is the result of the influences upon us merged with our experiences of life and the perceptions we have reasoned for ourselves – the **thought** element.

Let's look at each of the ego states before coming back to link the theory with assertiveness.

## YOUR PARENT EGO STATE

Imagine that from the day you were born until the age of about ten, a tape recorder was switched on inside your head to record everything that it hears from the outside world. Now, find yourself a quiet moment in your surroundings and in your head. Allow yourself to travel on a journey backwards. If you press the PLAY button now on that old tape recording, whose voices will you hear most? Maybe it is one or both of your actual parents, a teacher, a relative, a family friend, an older brother or sister?

What sort of messages will be on your recording from birth to about ten? Try to recall and note down some of the actual phrases which you can hear:

PERSON              SAYING
example; mother     *Don't show yourself up.*
example; teacher    *We've got high expectations of you.*
                    *Your brother did very well at this school.*

Your examples . . .

It is likely that you have heard a variety of messages; perhaps you could go back to what you've written and differentiate between those which are *positive* and those which are *negative* messages. Some of the messages may be neutral. Put a circle round those which you perceive to be negative.

Which do you hear most on the tape? Positive? Negative? Neutral?

Below are some of the typical responses to this exercise – how do they compare with what you have written?

*don't do that – do as you're told – you're a clever boy – because I said so – who do you think you are – well done – you should know better – never trust a . . . – wait till your father gets home – put your face straight – don't let the family down – don't show yourself up – don't, you'll hurt yourself – you must share – big boys don't cry – learn to stick up for yourself – don't raise your voice to me – I love you – always be polite to your elders – never go out looking untidy – you're so clumsy*

Many of the messages which you have been hearing will be *don't* and *do* messages laying down rules, probably with little, or no explanation. Some will be cautionary – '*mind you don't fall*', '*watch the road*', and some will be instructive – '*be polite*', '*be nice and share*'. Many of those you remember clearly are likely to be critical of you and may have been internalized as part of your belief system about life and about yourself.

The messages which have been recorded form a strong part of our personality and influence our behaviour as adults in two major ways – **re-playing the messages to ourselves** and **communicating the messages to others.**

## RE-PLAYING YOUR *PARENT* MESSAGES TO YOURSELF

Cast your mind back to the exercise you did in Chapter 5 on your positive qualities. Did it feel like there was somebody looking over your shoulder saying 'you shouldn't boast', 'don't show off', 'who do you think you are?' If you did feel this then it is likely that your own parent ego state was re-playing a message which has been frequently recorded for you. The voices on these recordings are people to whom we looked for wisdom and authority when we were forming our own self-image. If they told us frequently that we weren't clever enough, that we should control ourselves rather than show emotions, that we mustn't question authority, or that we were a nuisance – then those messages are likely to have influenced how we feel about ourselves as adults. This often makes us harder on ourselves than we are on other people, finding it difficult to be forgiving or accepting of our own shortcomings.

One way we re-play our negative parental messages is through the '*I Should/I Must*' game – it goes something like this:

*I Should be fitter*
*I Must ask so-and-so round*
*I Should be nicer to my mother-in-law*
*I Must look as though I can cope*
*I Should clean out the garage*
*I Should go and visit so-and-so*
*I Must finish this before I sit down*
*I Must show them that I'm as good as they are*

Perhaps you would like to add some of your own *Musts* and *Shoulds*.

These serve to reinforce the set of values imposed on us through actual parental messages, even though we are now adults who are aware that not all of these rules and values are still relevant to our own life today. Many of these values are essential as a code of morality or as personal principles, others will help us to achieve and be successful in life. However, the negative aspects – which cause us to be too hard on ourselves – also continue to play.

**This gets in the way of being assertive. It stops us from confidently and rationally believing that we have the right to assert ourselves.**

Sue and David are a 'thirty-something' professional couple whose small baby was taken into hospital. The hospital staff were casual and uncommunicative. After several days there was a worrying lack of urgency and efficiency in the treatment. Sue and David, both confident, articulate people, were deeply anxious about their baby yet were reluctant to appear 'pushy' or critical in expressing concern to the hospital staff. The belief that doctors know best and that we must be grateful for anything nurses do because they are so overworked, actually held them back from questioning and expressing their alarm.

Parental messages regarding authority, polite behaviour and gratitude got in the way of the need to assertively question authority in the way both of these people would normally do in other aspects of their lives.

## Changing Negative Messages

When our 'internal tape recording' is playing to reinforce criticism which we have heard as children it lowers our self-esteem and confidence. Those negative messages which you identified earlier in the chapter serve to 'put you in your place' even though the place you are entitled to occupy now, as an adult, is very different from your status as a child. It is hardly surprising that you will find it difficult to express what you really think, feel and want from others if the parental message you keep hearing is telling you that you are unimportant, unworthy, a nuisance or not entitled to question others.

Penny, a woman of 45, had been a nurse since leaving school and was promoted to a management position in the hospital where she had always worked. She knew that she was technically capable of doing the job as over the years she had gained qualifications to the level of a masters degree, but she lacked the communication and presentation skills necessary for the high profile nature of this new role. Encouraged by her director, Penny embarked on a programme of self-development which included some training in various aspects of interpersonal skills, including assertiveness.

Intellectually, she did not learn very much that she wasn't already aware of. As you can appreciate, a ward sister must be highly competent in using interpersonal skills; with patients, their relatives, staff, consultants and the external hospital network.

What Penny did start to learn was that she had been assertive throughout her career and that she had the *right to be successful* – that she could attend meetings with consultants and express her viewpoint without hearing that old parental message about not boasting and 'knowing your place'.

## Exercise
*Go back to each of the critical messages which you circled on page 46 and ask yourself the following, making a note of your answers:*

- Is this true about me now?
- Do I sometimes re-play this message and allow it to influence the way I behave?
- This prevents me from being assertive because . . .
- I don't need to play this message any more because . . .

## SENDING *PARENT* MESSAGES TO OTHERS

When we communicate to other people we sometimes do so directly from our *parent ego state* – this is particularly likely when we are criticizing somebody. Rather than offering constructive feedback, we tend to come across as aggressive. There are a lot of absolute statements associated with this ego state: '*You have no right . . .*', '*You should be . . .*', '*You're always . . .*'

Can you think of a time when you have heard yourself saying something to a child and realized that the words and the tone of voice are exactly the same as those which you were once used to hearing?

I remember when one of my daughters first appeared wearing 'real' make-up. I found myself saying, 'What have you got that muck on your face for; you're pretty enough without it.' On reflection I found my response shocking. The words, and tone of voice exactly mimicked my grandmother. My rational, adult self knows that make-up can be fun, experimenting is part of being young and my reaction was a put-down.

In a work situation when senior people give out this sort of parental message to their staff, it causes feelings of humiliation and rebelliousness. Remember, the *parent* ego state is not to do with age or being an actual parent. It is one of the aspects of our personality which influences the way we are. Children and young people also can behave in the *parent* state; listen to small children playing . . . you will hear them communicating from their *parent* state, repeating messages which have been recorded on their tape.

**Write down some of the things you do or say now as an adult which you have copied from one of your parents or somebody who was influential in your childhood.**

It is from this ego state that we can appear to be

domineering or patronizing, and to put people down. As we have seen, the *parent* ego state is not always in line with the reality of the present. Furthermore, it neglects the fact that other people perceive life differently from us. Our *parent* tends to communicate from an assumption that only our perception is correct. The high expectations – The *Shoulds* and *Musts* of my *parent* ego state might not be relevant or compatible with other people's experience of *parent* messages.

Gerald had worked in engineering since leaving school. Now, at 43, he had been made redundant and found unemployment a devastating experience. He was willing to do any kind of work just to 'be useful' again, and started signing-on at the job centre. Gerald was horrified when he listened to some of the people there, hearing that they had never had a job and weren't really interested in any of the 'situations vacant' on display. Consequently his attitude to the people was unpleasant and abusive. He had no perception of the fact that not working was the norm for these people, as it had been for other people in their families when they were young. Their *parental* messages were quite different from Gerald's but he showed prejudice towards them and became more angry about his own situation – rather than accepting them at face value and assertively going about his own business.

*We do not see things as they are – we see things as we are.*

## HOW OUR *PARENT* CAN PREVENT US FROM BEING ASSERTIVE.

### Old habits die hard
Our *parent* ego state will sometimes make assertiveness

difficult because what we are trying to assert might not be what we really think *now*, but something that has become a habit. This is never more true than when we are actually parenting our own children. If we continue to give them rules, with little or no logical explanation, at some stage in their development these rules cause argument. Because they genuinely don't understand any reason for the rules they will start to confront and question our authority – backed to the wall, our *parent* ego state becomes even stronger and so a state of conflict emerges.

In work situations managers whose control of their staff is *parent* based, get the result of people merely doing as they are told rather than taking initiative and working creatively.

## COMMUNICATING IN THE PARENT EGO STATE

What people say and the way they say it can give us clues to the ego state from which they are speaking. When we are in our *parent* state we will have a tendency to sound like some of the following:

**Authoritarian** – This is the way things are

**Stubborn** – I'm not interested in your opinion

**Pompous** – In my day you wouldn't have got away with this

**Condescending** – I knew I should have done it myself

**Threatening** – You'd better put it right or else

**Controlling** – You will do as I say.

When we look at the *adult* ego state we will see that there is an assertive alternative to this hierarchical attitude.

## YOUR *CHILD* EGO STATE

Having explored your *parent* ego state you are now invited to think about the *child* aspect of this theory. We said that the *child* ego state is that which is determined by how we **felt** the world around us when we were very young, rather than what we thought about it. Imagine now that there was a second tape – recording what you were *feeling* during your early years, but not what you heard. Think about what it is like being a young person; what are the feelings experienced by toddlers and children?

Here are some examples:

*happy – sad – scared –* **excited** *– jealous – 'that's not fair' – compliant – manipulative –* **curious – frustrated** *– confused – sulky –* **angry – affectionate – loving** *– inferior – rebellious*

Add some of your own to these . . .

These feelings are still part of us; the blueprint exists within our self to re-experience these feelings. When faced with difficulties, criticisms, threats or a fun environment, our behaviour is triggered by one of these feelings.

## TWO ASPECTS OF CHILD – FREE CHILD AND ADAPTED CHILD

**Free child**

Each of us has a certain amount of both of these aspects of the *child* ego state. Go back to the words you used to describe feelings. Those words which are in bold type represent behaviour which comes from the *free child*. This is the part of us which is likely to be creative, to enjoy partying, to rebel against authority and to lose our temper. Allowing the *free child* to emerge occasionally offers a healthy response to the stresses and strains of life. When we take everything, including ourselves, too seriously we lose sight of some of the spontaneity of life.

People express their *free child* in different ways, for example: Singing – Dancing – Hugging – Laughing – Crying – Partying – Physical exercise – Showing affection – Making love – Indulging in the pleasure of food and drink – Giving presents – Shopping . . .

These can all be seen as ways in which we express the *free child* in us – where we experience life through our senses in much the same way as we did when we were actually children.

How do you express your *free child*?

Which of the above do you do regularly?

Which of them did you used to do but have got out of the habit of doing?

What else do you do which isn't included in these examples?

In what ways would the quality of your overall well-being improve if you found more time to enjoy some of these pleasures?

So, what are you going to do about this?

Being emotionally and physically expressive is part of being assertive. It demonstrates a positive attitude in which life, regardless of its difficulties and sadness, is seen as an opportunity, not a threat. After all, life is all we've actually got. If we live with one foot in the past (regretting) and one foot in the future (feeling anxious) then we miss the present. Much of the *free child* activity described above involves the here and now – being alive for the moment.

The examples above represent the positive aspects of the *free child*, but it is unrealistic not to mention that there are also some negative aspects which can get in the way of being assertive. When we were children, we may have given vent to anger, jealousy and frustration by striking out at another person or behaving manipulatively in some way. This spontaneous behaviour is likely to be non-assertive because it is totally selfish, having no regard for the rights and feelings of the other person. Whether it manifests itself in aggression or manipulation it will usually lead to difficult relationships. If the other person is also behaving from their *free child*, there is the possibility that you may have a good fight, get it out of your system and clear the air. But in more formal relationships this is rarely the way things happen. If you are interested in learning more about ego states and communication I recommend that you read some of the excellent books available on Transactional Analysis from the Recommended Further Reading section at the back of this book.

## Adapted child

The other aspect of the *child* ego state is influenced by the way we have learned to help ourselves feel more comfortable through adapting to other people's needs and expectations of us. If, as a small child, you were given rewards or 'positive strokes' for behaving in a gentle, quiet, unobtrusive way, then that is likely to be your general demeanour as an adult. Anger is an emotion which in our culture is seen as negative and 'naughty'. If you have been punished for showing and expressing anger then it is likely that you will have adapted that behaviour in order to avoid punishment. This can often lead to a sulky, sullen response to situations which we don't like or don't agree with. As we will see in Chapter 7, some people are very nervous of conflict. If, when you play the *feelings* tape recording from your childhood, there is fear and anxiety on that tape, then you are likely to avoid situations which might recall that state.

It is the *adapted child* ego state which evokes the desire to please others. Whilst this is a wonderful and generous trait, you know enough about assertiveness by now to see the alarm bells. Pleasing others is only possible if we are also able to please ourselves. Being able to say 'NO' and express our own needs is vital. The *adapted child* ego state contributes enormously to **passive** behaviour – what we must learn is that we are not the vulnerable child being threatened by big important people any more. We are thinking, capable grown-ups with rights, who are willing to accept other people's rights and work towards comfortable, compatible relationships.

William is a middle-aged insurance administrator. He is efficient and highly numerate but has constantly been overlooked for promotion. His employers describe him as honest, hard-working, dependable, and 'a whizz with figures'. Yet, after 16 years in the same job he has seen junior people overtake him to achieve promotions into jobs which he is technically capable of doing. During an appraisal with a new boss, it became clear that William lacked the confidence and self-assurance needed to compliment the technical aspects required for promotion to a more senior job in the company.

It transpired that William had missed a lot of schooling as a child due to his parents' lack of interest in education. When he did attend school he was faced with a particularly harsh form teacher who humiliated and taunted William by continually goading him to account for his absence. William had learned very astutely to stay out of authority's way, keep his head down and do the best he could. This is what he brought to his working life and this was how he was perceived by employers and colleagues. Of course they all described him as 'hard-working and dependable' – he never said 'NO' to anything and often took work home. William's *adapted child* ego state was prevalent and as an adult he continued to see people in authority as powerful. In their presence his feelings re-played the tape of fear and humiliation.

Try to recall a time when you, as a child, were subjected to this kind of experience – either from a parent, teacher, older child or another adult.

Can you remember and describe your feelings at the time?

Are there any situations which you now experience as an adult feeling like this?

Are there any people, or types of people who you still feel like this with?

What are you going to do to make sure that these very real and understandable feelings don't get in the way when you would like to present yourself assertively?

William's manager sent him on an Assertiveness Training Course, where he learned to look at his strengths and to role-play situations in which he stood up to people who were supposedly more clever and powerful than himself.

'Nobody *can make you feel inferior without your permission.*'
**Eleanor Roosevelt**

## COMMUNICATING IN THE *CHILD* EGO STATE

When we are in our *child* ego state we will have a tendency to sound like some of the following:

**Complaining, moaning, whining** – That's not fair
**Challenging** – Mine's better than yours
**Demanding** – I want . . .
**Bargaining** – I will if you will
**Sulking** – It's not my fault
**Angry** – Slamming doors, stamping feet
**Complying** – All right then
Which of these do you hear yourself saying?

When, in the adult world, we are faced with situations where, subconsciously, we re-experience our child-like feelings, we behave in our *child* state. This explains why we occasionally react in a manner which is totally disproportionate to what is actually happening. Something triggers feelings of threat, humiliation, anger or sense of unfairness and we behave in ways rather like a grown-up equivalent of lying down on the supermarket floor screaming, or taking our ball away so that nobody else can play!

## YOUR *ADULT* EGO STATE

The *adult* ego state is probably what you operate in most of the time. It is the part of us which has thought about and learned from experiences – that has formed our own framework and attitudes to how we live our lives and how we accept other people. Our *adult* state is not judgmental of others, it accepts our own fallibility and takes account of our own and other people's rights. The *adult* element responds to what is actually going on – it is a rational response to behaviour based on taking in the messages that are being transmitted here and now. This ego state relies on knowledge and experience; it helps us to behave objectively.

It is the *adult* ego state which enables us to behave

61

assertively, not requiring that we defend ourselves or attack somebody else.

## COMMUNICATING IN THE *ADULT* EGO STATE

When we are in our *adult* ego state, we will probably use some of the following:

**Reasoning** – I see your point of view

**Problem-solving** – What do you think is the way forward here?

**Disclosing** – I am upset and disappointed about this

**Making criticism** – My view is that it wasn't handled well

**Clarifying** – Can I check if we both see this the same way?

Now compare how more assertive these examples are than those written for the *parent* and the *child* ego states.

### Exercise
*As a test to see how well you have understood this explanation of Transactional Analysis, try to identify from which ego state each of the following statements have been made:*

1. 'This is a load of rubbish, I've got by all my life without learning about this TA business.'
2. 'This sounds interesting. I wonder if it can offer a new approach to solving a personality clash which is going on at work at the moment?'
3. 'I'd better learn about this in case the person who lent me this book expects me to have an intelligent discussion about it.'
4. 'I'm going to read a bit more about this, I think it could be helpful to me.'

5. 'Whoopee, does this mean it's all right for me to get drunk at the office party this year!'

ANSWERS: 1. *Parent*; 2. *Adult*; 3. *Adapted Child*; 4. *Adult*; 5. *Free Child*

**A healthy individual needs a mixture of all three ego states to take them successfully through life's journey.**

Your *parent* state is the basic map on which the routes, dangers and opportunities are written. Sometimes, the map will be out of date making it necessary to question it by exploring routes from the thinking, reasoning and objectivity which is your *adult*. Your *child* state is your experience of the journey; the willingness to delight in the opportunities, explore new territories, risk new approaches and feel the emotions of living.

Understanding more about ourselves gives us more choices about how we can behave – strengthening our *adult* aspects increases our ability to be assertive. The aim of TA is to increase our *adult* state but in doing so, don't obliterate the *child* or *parent* states; it is sufficient to be aware of them, and be able to acknowledge that the behaviour which is routed in one of those ego states might not always be appropriate for the situation at the time.

## I'M OK – YOU'RE OK

In developing Berne's TA theory, Thomas Harris describes what has come to be known as the OK CORRAL. Basically there are four 'life positions' which we can adopt:

| I'm OK | I'm OK |
|---|---|
| You're *not* OK | You're OK |
| Often results in putting others down; needing to *show them* who is *best*. Lacking in self-confidence and self-esteem. | Accepts that I am not perfect and neither are you. Respects self and others. |
| I'm *not* OK | I'm *not* OK |
| You're OK | You're *not* OK |
| Because others are seen as *better* you give your power away to them (and sure enough, they will take it). | Extreme lack of self-worth and loss of interest in life. |

## CHAPTER 6 SUMMARY

- The theory of TA is another tool we can use to help us understand why we behave in certain ways with certain people.
- The *parent* ego state is about what we have been **taught**; the *child* is what we have **felt** and the *adult* is what we have **thought** and **reasoned**.
- We all have the capacity for change – we don't have to react as we did when we were children, neither do we have to still believe rigidly everything that we were told about ourselves or the world around us.
- We are no better or worse than other people, merely different.
- Assertiveness is I'm OK – You're OK – respecting yourself and the other person.

# CHAPTER 7

# Handling conflict

## CONFLICT AND YOU

**Exercise**

|  | Seldom | Sometimes | Frequently |
|---|---|---|---|
| 1. Do you shy away from conflict, seeing it as dangerous and fraught with potential pain? | | | |
| 2. Do you become distressed when you are around people who are arguing or shouting at one another? | | | |
| 3. Can you contradict a domineering person? | | | |
| 4. Do you express your opinions if they differ from those held by others? | | | |
| 5. If you feel someone is being unfair do you say so? | | | |
| 6. If you are interrupted do you make any comment? | | | |

If you have answered 'Frequently' to the first two questions and 'Seldom' or 'Sometimes' to the others, then it suggests that you see conflict as a danger zone which you would avoid entering. If this is your view of conflict then you probably tend to avoid dealing with contentious issues by either bypassing the people involved, sweeping things under the carpet in the hope that they might go away or even participating in some *stamp collecting*. Does this sound like you? If you do *appear* to go through life avoiding conflict with other people then I suspect that the inner conflict you experience is rather turbulent.

On the other hand, if you have answered 'Seldom' to the first two questions and 'Frequently' to the others then it suggests that you are assertive. A word of caution though, if you have answered this way because you *seek out* conflict and use it maliciously in order to ensure that you have the upper hand, then you are actually showing a tendency to be aggressive. Is this true of you? If so, then you too probably suffer from inner turbulence. What's it like being alone with yourself in a quiet room? Do you like the person you are with? If you experience that uncomfortable feeling of having to justify yourself and your behaviour it may be a sign that you have behaved badly in a conflict situation.

If you are usually in the middle of these two polarities then it is likely that you generally deal with conflict in an assertive way.

Like death, taxes and change, conflict is an inevitable part of life – **it does not have to be synonymous with crisis**. It does not necessarily involve entering a danger zone where either you are going to get hurt or you are going to hurt somebody else. *Conflict is inevitable; a fight is a choice.*

Maintaining an *I'm OK – You're OK* stance is never

more important than when we are faced with conflict. Remember, there doesn't have to be a winner or a loser, what is needed is resolution of the problem. Sadly, because they find conflict so threatening, people tend to avoid it and issues don't become resolved. '*Least said, soonest mended*' is a phrase which I recently heard from somebody who had been very badly treated in front of a group of colleagues. The person left the situation feeling humiliated and hurt but unwilling to say anything; his explanation: 'once I let it all out the consequences might be dire.' This is a typical response to conflict situations. The perception is that the only outcome will be full-scale strife – a dangerous and potentially painful arena which is to be avoided at all cost. On the other hand, the person who had lashed out at this man was unrepentant and rather self-congratulatory: 'I like to put the cat among the pigeons now and then and get people going, they should speak up for themselves if they don't like it' he responded. Clearly he wasn't disturbed by the situation and remains comfortable in the 'strife arena' holding his position – *I'm OK – You're not OK* – in this relationship.

It is important to understand that people have different approaches and attitudes to conflict. Feeling affronted because people don't behave as we think they **should** can get in the way of moving nearer to understanding the person's point and trying to find a resolution. Sometimes we need to acknowledge to ourselves that we are hurt and then deal with the pain. Allowing ourselves to feel that pain is often the first step to healing. It is essential to come to terms with the fact that we have to deal with non-assertive behaviour from other people, however assertive we ourselves might have become.

## POSITIVE APPROACHES TO CONFLICT

Conflict doesn't have to hurt; sometimes it can stimulate change, clear the air and open up new perspectives in a relationship. Too much conformity in groups and families can lead to stagnation, ritual and avoidance of change. We have only one life – to live it in a rut is something of a waste. The positive aspects of conflict should not be overlooked in order to maintain a quiet life. Current management thinking advocates conflict as a feature of a *learning* organization. Cosy consensus is seen to stifle people and obstruct creativity.

## POSITIVE ASPECTS OF CONFLICT

- It lays problems out on the table and opens up discussion
- It can lead to solutions and a happier outcome for all
- It increases communication between people and leads to greater mutual understanding
- It gives the opportunity to explore problems and find creative solutions
- It releases emotions which have been hidden away
- It can be great fun making up!

## TWO ELEMENTS OF COMMUNICATION – CONTENT AND BEHAVIOUR

**Focusing on the content**
There are two aspects to communication: the **content** – what is being said; and the **behaviour** – the way it is being said. Most of the time we are more influenced by

the behaviour of the person than by what they are actually saying to us.

Imagine the same lecture being delivered by two different people. The first one walks into the room, sets out his notes and proceeds to read the content in a monotone, making little effort to acknowledge the audience in front of him. The second person walks into the room, scans the audience, makes a warm greeting and delivers the content, varying her voice, pausing at strategic points and creating rapport with the people to whom she is delivering the lecture. Which of the two is going to succeed in getting more of the message across? In each case the CONTENT is identical but the BEHAVIOUR will strongly influence the listeners.

*Now imagine you have just made a suggestion about a way to tackle something.*

- **First response:** 'Well, that idea has its merits, but I don't think that it's likely to achieve the outcome we're looking for.'
- **Second response:** 'Oh come on, that's a stupid idea, you know that has no chance of working at all!'

Although the first person is disagreeing with you, you will probably accept their comments and continue to go forward with a rational discussion. The second response is likely to result in you either backing down or retaliating aggressively and getting into a battle. In fact, the **content** is the same in both instances; it is the **behaviour** which is different and it is the behaviour which evokes the response. The most appropriate reply to **either** of these is something like 'OK, it was just a thought. What's your suggestion?' in a calm, assertive voice. When we respond negatively to the behaviour we allow our own response to be determined by the other person's behaviour.

Remember the effect of the PARENT-CHILD ego state relationships which were outlined in the previous chapter. To deal assertively with conflict we must be influenced by the content of the discussion, not contaminated by the behaviour of the other person or people. That way we remain in control of the situation by avoiding becoming either personally attacked, or attacking the other person back in retaliation.

**Exercise**
*Try to observe other people in your own social, family or work circles to see how they handle conflict situations. You will start to recognize quite clearly how responding to behaviour actually makes the conflict more difficult to resolve. Television programmes, particularly some soaps, are also very useful for observing the consequences of behaviour. If you needed an excuse to watch the soaps then you can now put it down to personal development!*

**Techniques involved in conflict handling are:**
* LISTENING NON-EMOTIONALLY
* LISTENING TO THE CONTENT RATHER THAN THE BEHAVIOUR
* FOCUSING THE DISCUSSION ON THE CONTENT

**and then if necessary:**
* DISCUSSING THE BEHAVIOUR AND THE EFFECT IT IS HAVING
* LISTENING NON-EMOTIONALLY involves staying **objective** about what is being said and the way it is being said. The problem is that once our emotions become involved the tendency is to start 'joining in' with either defensive or attacking behaviour. If your

self-esteem is healthy, then it is easier to listen without being influenced emotionally.

- LISTENING TO THE CONTENT means concentrating on what is being said, not the way it is being said. It enables you to have a greater understanding of the real issue and to assess the importance and merits of what is being discussed. Don't forget, some people find it very difficult to be assertive. Just because you have become better at it don't expect the same from everybody. As we have discussed, people might handle a situation of conflict aggressively because inside they feel nervous and uncomfortable about it.

- FOCUSING THE DISCUSSION ON THE CONTENT – rather than becoming involved in the way the person is behaving towards you. This often serves to diffuse the situation and brings the other person into line with a more objective approach to the issue.

however . . .

- DISCUSSING THE BEHAVIOUR AND THE EFFECT IT IS HAVING – on you and on the discussion – might become necessary. If you are really not getting anywhere it is useful to move from CONTENT to PROCESS. This means departing from the actual issue in order to discuss what is going on between you. For example: '*We don't seem to be making any progress; it seems to me that every time I mention my solution you change the subject or refuse to discuss it.*'

In this situation one person appears to be blocking the progress of discussion, prompting the speaker to attempt to bring to the surface and deal with underlying issues. Whilst this may be seen as confrontational and likely to spark off conflict, it is actually a positive approach to take the issue – and probably the relationship – into a deeper level of dialogue and ultimately, understanding.

Does this strike you as risky? Do you do this? Have you ever done this? Will you do this when faced with a stalemate situation where both parties are locked into a paralysis of disagreement? Remember, the speaker would be using an assertive style of communication, taking responsibility for his viewpoint, speaking in a calm, controlled voice and giving the other person time and space to put their point across. The purpose is to encourage the other person to open up, **not to arouse them into behaving defensively.**

In a meeting, changing **content** to **process** might go like this:

*'There are a lot of silences and raised eyebrows around the table. We seem to have hit a raw nerve with a few people. I would like to clear the air a bit and find out what the underlying issues really are here.'*

This can avoid the destructive practice, common in meetings, where people withhold their thoughts and feelings and then leave the meeting talking about why it won't work or why they won't comply.

By shifting focus from content to process we are looking at behaviour constructively rather than destructively. This is an assertive way of ensuring that people are encouraged to express what they really think and want.

A crude, but sometimes essential use of the **CONTENT to PROCESS** technique is to say, calmly, but as loudly as necessary in order to be heard : 'I cannot think clearly whilst you are yelling at me.'

# THE FOUR-PART ASSERTIVE RESPONSE
# TO CONFLICT

## 1. APPROPRIATENESS OF ENVIRONMENT

You have choices. There might be reasons for not getting into discussion with this person (or this group) at this time, in this place. Would it be better to arrange another time or move into a different setting? Where are you physically positioned? If you are at a disadvantage, such as sitting with somebody standing over you, then maybe you need to stand up and move away to create equal height and comfortable distance. The more you can 'stage-manage' the setting, the more confident, comfortable and in control you will be.

## 2. ACTIVE LISTENING

This involves more than just hearing what is being said, or waiting for the other person to finish. Active listening involves:

- putting yourself in a position where you can *hear* clearly.
- *concentrating* on the speaker and the content of what they are saying.
- *acknowledging* that you have heard.
- *clarifying* points to check that you have understood.

## 3. EXPRESSING YOURSELF

This means putting forward what you think and, where appropriate, what your feelings are. Letting somebody know your views does not necessarily have to be contentious, telling them how you feel about the issue does not necessarily mean making yourself vulnerable. Of course this will depend on the circumstances. It is essential to be in control of your own boundaries by choosing

73

how much of your feelings you wish to reveal. But how will they ever know if you don't tell them?

## 4. SAYING WHAT YOU WOULD LIKE TO HAPPEN OR HOW YOU WOULD LIKE THINGS TO BE

This will usually be easier to do if you have had time to think it through. I think this is often the trickiest part of conflict – it is harder to actually state what we do want than what we don't want. People are often geared up to express what they are angry or unhappy about, but blow it by being unable to state clearly what they want from the other person.

- **Firstly** we must accept that there is a possibility that we won't get what we want; remember, the other person has rights, too. If you are open enough to acknowledge this to yourself then it becomes less of a battle, you are more prepared for a **WIN/WIN** solution.
- **Secondly**, the speaker should be calm and respectful. This means ensuring that you are taking personal responsibility for what you are saying and acknowledging the other person's rights.

## COMPROMISE

In order to reach a WIN/WIN outcome to conflict we must be prepared to accept that everybody has certain rights in any situation. If we win and the other person loses then maybe they will become determined to seek revenge some day. On the other hand, if we lose and the other person wins we can develop a *You're OK – I'm not OK* attitude with that person. Winning the actual issue isn't the only aspect of a situation; retaining your self-respect and respecting the other person is also important. Finding a way which is reasonably agreeable to both parties – some form of workable compromise – is more likely to leave doors open and build positive relationships.

However, whilst compromise is an important aspect of assertiveness, it is important not to compromise yourself. If you strongly disagree with somebody on the grounds of ethics, morals or principles then you should explain yourself and stay close to what you believe in.

## BUILD GOLDEN BRIDGES OVER WHICH YOUR ENEMY CAN RETREAT

Imagine you are in a hurry. You need to go to the bank, it is busy in town and you decide to park on a yellow line, knowing you will only be a few minutes. As you turn the corner to return to your car there is a traffic warden writing out a ticket. You are angry, with yourself of course, and feel hard done by. Naturally you will probably 'have a go' at talking your way out of the ticket. No chance. The traffic warden is doing her job. You have choices here – either you can snatch the ticket, utter offensive remarks and storm off, or you can look the warden in the eye, say 'fair enough, but you can't blame me for trying' and take the ticket gracefully. Assertive people don't always get their own way you know!

When a potential conflict situation arises in your life, give some thought to these questions:

1. What will I gain from avoiding this conflict?
2. What will my personal costs be if I avoid this conflict?

3. What will be the longer-term consequences of 1 and 2?
4. How would I like the long-term picture of my relationship to look in this case?
5. Do I have the right to resolve this conflict situation?

Possible answers might be:

1. *The chance to go on feeling aggrieved and thinking I am right, they are wrong.*
2. *Having to avoid certain subjects and swallow my opinions.*
3. *The building of a bigger barrier which will prevent us ever really co-operating.*
4. *Being more relaxed and open; able to say what I do and don't agree with.*
5. *Yes; as long as I do it assertively and sensitively.*

Working through this process of self-awareness helps to put a clear understanding of the risks of either acting or not acting in any situation. It may result in a decision to do nothing because that is preferable, but at least you will know the consequences and have decided to live with them. If the result is that you *do* decide to take action then refer back to the FOUR-PART response on pages 73-74.

If you are initiating some discussion which is potentially fraught with conflict it can be helpful to start it with something like . . . 'I want to say something to you. It is important to me and I've got a lot of feelings about it, so it might not come out very well. Please will you give me a chance to say what I want to say.' (There is a scene in the movie *The American President* where Annette Benning does this beautifully.)

We have already mentioned appropriateness of

environment. Sometimes it is easier to say difficult things when you don't have to 'eyeball' the other person – inviting them to walk with you for a while or driving along in a car can be useful tactics to make the situation less tense or embarrassing. Social workers who work with adolescents find that an effective way of helping them to open up and express themselves is to take them out in a car or get them to help with some physical task. They feel less under pressure to talk than in an office or counselling room situation.

## DIFFERENT PEOPLE – DIFFERENT SITUATIONS

Make a note of the people who you *do* find it difficult to be in conflict with and those you *don't*.

Now note down situations where you would flee like a lamb from conflict and those where you would stay and fight like a lion.

Are there any obvious patterns which emerge here?

Is it to do with ego states and feelings of OK or not OK?

What can you do to shift your feelings to a more comfortable *I'm OK – You're OK* attitude in order to deal with the situation in your *adult* state?

Remember you have rights and so does the other person. You can choose how you respond to conflict.

Sometimes it is necessary to behave like a lion rather than a lamb.

## CHAPTER 7 SUMMARY

• Conflict does not necessarily mean crisis or a danger zone to be avoided at all cost.

- Conflict can be creative and take relationships to a better level of understanding.
- Concentrate on the CONTENT rather than the behaviour of the other person.
- Practise the FOUR-PART assertive response to conflict.
- Understand more about yourself and conflict.
- A workable compromise can offer a WIN/WIN solution.

# CHAPTER 8

# Being an assertive consumer

Over the past decade our society has become increasingly consumerist. When we go to see our dentist, we are the customer, if we sign on at the job centre we are the customer and hospitals increasingly refer to patients as customers. Managers are told that their staff are their customers. Civil servants are given Customer Care Training in order to meet the requirements of the Citizens' Charter. Whatever your view on this development, it brings a change in focus and emphasis which we need to learn to deal with. My view is that generally, British people are not very skilled at being customers; is this because we are *subjects* not *citizens*? Neither are we particularly disposed towards giving service – is it something to do with our class system that suggests servility is demeaning?

When I first visited the USA and Australia I was taken aback by the greetings in shops and restaurants. At first, the 'Hi, how are you today?' seemed really strange; I wanted to look behind me to see if they were actually talking to somebody else. It made me wonder if, in the UK, there is a fleeting moment in which we assess the status of a stranger before we decide how we will treat them. Do we make an assessment about whether we are in a superior or inferior position to them before we begin communication?

Although this idea suggests a cynicism which I am uncomfortable about, nevertheless it does bear out some of my experience of being a customer and also of training people in the skills of customer service.

### Consumer rights

As a customer, it is important to be aware of consumer rights and to take responsibility to ensure that we get what we pay for. There are numerous books, publications, radio and television programmes to help us with this. I have found the local Trading Standards Office or Citizens Advice Bureau useful. Their numbers can be found in local telephone directories. Also, many large organizations now publish a 'Customer Charter' or 'Customer Promise' leaflet telling us the standards we should expect and advising how to complain if standards are not met. It is not these formal procedures which this chapter will deal with, but the subtleties of ensuring you get a satisfactory service – something I believe can be achieved through an assertive approach.

## THE HUMAN FACTOR

Television programmes relating horror stories about how people have been treated; whether by builders, restaurants, airlines, hospitals – the list is numerous – have become increasingly popular. I believe they encourage us to complain and assert our rights. Unfortunately though, they don't teach how to do it assertively.

Next time you go into a shop, before making your enquiry, try preceding it with a smile and a greeting: *'Good afternoon. I wonder if you can help me, I'm look-*

*ing for a . . .'* Maybe this sounds rather like the first lesson of a foreign language evening class. I don't mean to be patronizing. I firmly believe that this short greeting gets us off to a better start by showing respect to the salesperson, assistant or receptionist. I feel that it is even more necessary when we are going to make a complaint. The ethos is that of *I'm OK – You're OK* and we are coming together from different angles to meet a need – *Not* that we are opponents prepared for battle.

*'No challenge should be faced without a little charm and a lot of style.'*
The Bluetones

## YOU HAVE THE RIGHT TO ASK

Good customer service involves being able to deal well with **people** and also having efficient **procedures**. As a customer, there are occasions when we don't know the procedure or the hidden rules of an organization, and people working there can sometimes make us feel stupid or inferior because we are not aware of how things work. Simple things like queuing systems, self-service machines or terminology, can cause us to feel foolish if we allow them to. It is all right not to know, despite the fact that the people serving might treat you as an imbecile. If a receptionist looks over her glasses at you saying *'of course you can't have an appointment straight away'*, or somebody tells you that a door you have just walked through is private, it is not your fault. The organization has the responsibility to make procedures and rules clear to their customers.

If, as a family, you go out to eat in a pub or restaurant it is useful to know how long it takes between ordering your food and receiving it. In my experience, staff tend to be defensive about this when you make the enquiry and rarely give you a truthful answer. You have the right to know. If kids are hungry they don't enjoy lingering over a drink whilst their meal is being cooked. All you need to know is whether you should buy them some crisps or ask for some bread, or will the meal be here in five minutes! I have learned to preface my enquiry with 'I'm not hustling you, just asking, how long is it likely to be before our meal arrives?' Maybe you see this as unnecessary thinking that you shouldn't have to make yourself amenable to the waiter/waitress – I see it as removing misunderstanding and tempering assertiveness with a little gentility.

Because the general public are becoming increasingly more demanding and often even abusive, people in service jobs tend – sometimes necessarily – to be armed for combat; it is helpful to identify yourself as neutral so that they know you are not the enemy.

## ESTABLISHING A CUSTOMER-PROVIDER RELATIONSHIP

I have used the term 'neutral' because there is a danger of becoming over-friendly and clouding the relationship of customer/supplier. If we become personally familiar then it is more difficult to put things right if they go wrong.

Think about a time when you have had workmen in your home. You start off quite friendly, making them cups of tea, hearing about how their children are doing at school, finding yourself telling them things about your own life. After a while this can evolve into something which is rather more than you want. Your time is being taken up, their tea breaks get longer and you come back from the shops to find them using your phone. Tricky. There is, by definition, something personal about them being in your home, anyway. But they are *not* guests, they are there to perform a specific task for which you have paid an agreed sum. Later in this chapter there is a questionnaire which will take you through a process of contract planning which can help you to avoid the situation which I have just described.

## Moaners and Groaners

As a customer we have rights, as a human being we also have responsibilities. The disease of moaning and whinging but not actually taking positive steps to put things right feeds low-esteem and contaminates our life. It obstructs the positive attitude required for assertive behaviour and contributes to many people's *stamp collection*.

I was recently on an Intercity train. Halfway into my journey there was a strong smell of burning and within a few minutes we had pulled into a station and been told to leave the train. Almost immediately, people who had avoided eye contact or conversation with one another for hours were united in their rally cry of 'typical', 'this is ridiculous,' etc., etc. Almost everybody around me was moaning, yet I felt that it was far preferable to be standing on an airy platform than travelling at high speed in a train which could be potentially dangerous.

Moaning about, and belittling certain services has become a kind of sport for people to indulge in. Maybe having a collective snipe helps people to feel less powerless. I am not suggesting that we should accept bad service or put up with not getting value for our money – I am suggesting that we have the capacity to differentiate between bad service and accidental incidents.

The Johnson family had saved hard for their holiday in Tenerife. They had spent a lot of time poring over brochures to make the right choice of hotel. During the first night of their stay they were disturbed by a variety of noises; this continued on the following nights and it was soon clear that the room they were in was badly designed and would always be subject to noise disturbance.

The family spent their two-week holiday feeling aggrieved and bemoaning their fate to any other residents who would listen. They 'didn't want to upset things' so they did not make a complaint to the hotel or ask to be moved. Consequently they had a miserable holiday, feeling disappointed and angry. They were ratty with one another about the problem and all sorts of other dissatisfactions surfaced about their relationships and their life in general. The hotel may have been aware that the room was below standard but were allowed to get away with it because nobody asked them to do anything. The Johnsons were utterly passive guests/customers.

When they arrived home their neighbour told them that they would be able to claim compensation. Suddenly Mr and Mrs Johnson became very active consumers by writing an indignant letter to the holiday company. Apart from the room problem, they threw in a few other dissatisfactions for good measure in the hope of getting even more compensation. Of course, they did not receive anything other than a letter of apology from the Customer Service department. As they had not registered any complaint at the time they were not entitled to anything else. Even if they had been awarded some financial compensation, they couldn't have got their time back, could they?

**Horses for Courses (or you get what you pay for)**

At the other end of the spectrum, I recently sat next to somebody on a flight who behaved as though she had bought a first-class ticket even though she was travelling in economy. She made constant demands of the cabin staff, complained about the quality of the food, requested extra pillows and blankets and rang the attendant bell to ask questions about the journey, temperature at our destination and, seemingly, anything else she could think of to make a nuisance of herself. You could say that she was asserting herself and ensuring that she got good service, but I say that she was taking advantage of the cabin crew and demanding more than she was actually entitled to.

There is a compromise between these two examples of consumer behaviour. We have the right to get value for money, but we have the responsibility to ensure that we know what we have paid for. If you eat in Joe's Café then you are entitled to receive the service and product promised for the price – the same applies if you eat at the Ritz.

## THE CUSTOMER ISN'T ALWAYS RIGHT

It is impossible to be truly assertive if you are not being truthful. The first honesty must be with yourself. Being assertively in control of your life should actually help you to discern between things you actually want and things which glossy advertising tells you that you are supposed to want.

Face it, a new 'dream' kitchen is unlikely to make your house bigger, your home happier, or you a better cook. It will fulfil certain needs but when you are buying, it is your responsibility to determine your needs in order to buy well and appropriately. Nit-picking after you have made a purchase because basically you made the wrong decision is not assertive.

- Be sure that you are buying for the right reasons and that you know what you need or want the product to fulfil.
- If you are dissatisfied, then the cause of your complaint must be a fault with the product or service, not the decision or choice which you have made.

## STAY IN CONTROL

High-pressure, fast-talking selling is outdated – when confronted with it we usually hear alarm bells which give us the opportunity to either avoid or slow down the sales pitch. However, there are other tactics and approaches used in sales which make us vulnerable. Once you start to feel yourself wanting to buy something because the sales assistant is 'so nice', 'really helpful' or 'seems genuinely interested in me', beware. If these *contribute* to your choice to buy then fine, but if they become your *reason for buying* then you need to take stock of your feelings.

Can you recall a time when, even as you arrive at the till transaction stage, or maybe when you have got the goods home, you have felt a slight unease that you've been seduced by the assistant rather than the product?

**You can say NO – the situation is not personal, it is a business deal**
Whether they are being calculatingly manipulative or they are genuinely interested in you, an astute sales person can hook your emotions so that you want to please them by buying their products.

**Useful tactics for staying in control in these situations:**

- Calculate how long it takes you to earn that money
- Think about how often you will actually use/wear/ benefit from the item
- Imagine the sales assistant in your position, think how in control they are likely to be as a customer
- Remember that if you say 'NO' you will be just as important when you walk out of that shop as you were when you walked in

## THE RULES

If you have purchased goods or services which do not meet their promise then you have the right to complain. If something is faulty, then provided you return it to the place where you bought it within a 'reasonable time of purchase', you have every right to expect a refund.

If you have worn, washed, taken apart or further damaged the faulty goods yourself in any way, this may affect your right to a full refund.

If you buy something and then decide that you don't want the goods, the vendor is under no obligation to refund your money or offer you a replacement. Where this does happen it is the policy of the business and is carried out as goodwill rather than legal transaction.

Most of the larger stores now give refunds for unwanted goods as a standard customer service policy. Everybody knows that if you buy something from Marks & Spencer and you still have the receipt then you are entitled to a full cash refund. This is the company's policy, it is the way they do business, yet it is amusing to stand and watch people's behaviour when they are returning goods. For example:

- *'My aunt bought this for me and it doesn't fit.'*
- *'When I got it home it didn't go with the trousers.'*
- *'I bought it for a friend and she didn't like it.'*

For some reason people appear to feel guilty about what they are doing and have to make an excuse. It is not necessary to do this. It is allowed, it's in the rules, you are not being naughty. If people feel that they must do this in a place where it is made easy to return goods, no wonder they find it difficult in less amenable places. This offers you a good starting-place to practise your 'assertive customer' skills.

*If, in the past, you have been one of those people who always felt they need to give an excuse or explanation then have a go at doing it differently.*

Walk up to the desk, smile at the assistant, take the goods and receipt from the bag and say 'I'd like a cash refund please'. Nothing else, just that. Take the money, say 'thank you', and go. That's all there is to it!

## RETURNING FAULTY GOODS

### Attitude

At the beginning of this chapter I talked about approach and using a bit of charm. This is never more necessary than when you are going to make a complaint. To begin with, if you go in with all guns blazing then a salesperson is likely to 'take you on'. This might mean sticking rigidly to procedures and going by the book. If your opening gambit is 'I want to speak to the manager' then the salesperson might see the need to watch his/her back and be defensive or obstructive. Like any situation of conflict, once personal attacks start, it is difficult to separate content from behaviour and things get out of hand. If the salesperson sees you as amenable then they will usually be willing to discuss the problem in order to help find a solution. If you don't get satisfaction from the salesperson then it is appropriate to ask to see a supervisor or decision-maker.

## Preparation

- Plan what you want to say before launching into your complaint
- Rehearse the story if it is complicated
- Decide what outcome will be acceptable to you
- Be clear about the details of guarantees or contract agreements
- Take a deep breath and remind yourself that you have the right to get what you pay for
- Open the conversation with a greeting – announce what you are there for and check that you are speaking to the appropriate person
- If you prefer not to have an audience, ask if there is somewhere private where you can discuss your business
- Stay in control of your feelings – this is not a personal issue for either side involved

## Opening Gambit

If you begin a complaint in a timid voice, saying 'I'm awfully sorry to trouble you' then it is likely that the person to whom you are complaining will subconsciously start to dismiss the importance of what you are saying. Go back to your plan and remind yourself of your rights. You don't want the other person to think you are a pushover from the beginning. You can remain calm, pleasant and respectful even though you are determined to achieve your outcome. There is no doubt that we are judged by appearance and also that we are influenced by how good we *think* we look. If you are going to make a complaint give some thought to how you are going to present yourself. Like it or not, people are impressionable and they are more likely to take notice of you if you look well-groomed, organized and confident.

Being a customer can be hard work. Sometimes I let things go because I don't feel up to it, see that the front-line person is already under pressure or decide that I don't want to spend time giving somebody feedback on their lack of customer service provision. Once again, if this is your choice then it's fine. But don't be like the Johnsons and spoil precious time by moaning.

## The broken record

This is possibly the most widely known assertive technique. Basically it is about deciding on the outcome you want and repeating a statement continuously until you get it! Children are naturally excellent at the broken record: 'Can I go to the park?', 'Please let me go to the park', 'Oh go on, let me go to the park' and so it goes on. Have you been beaten down by this technique? If so, you're in good company. Research on analysis of conversations where this technique is used shows that in the majority of situations the person using the *broken record* technique gets their way.

Picture the following scenario: Mike bought a pair of shoes a week ago and the stitching has come undone. They have not been subjected to abnormal wear and he has a good case for asking for a refund. He doesn't want a replacement as he is not confident that the same thing won't happen again.

Customer: *Good morning, I bought these shoes here last week and the stitching has come undone. Here is my receipt and I would like a refund please.*

Assistant: *We don't give refunds I'm afraid, but I can replace the shoes for you.*
Customer: **Thank you, but I don't want another pair. I have my receipt and I would like a refund please.**
Assistant: *Our policy is to replace shoes if we've got them in stock.*
Customer: **I understand that that is your policy but I have my receipt and I would like a refund please.**
Assistant: *The manager isn't here this morning. I can't give you a refund.*
Customer: **I understand that is a problem for you but I would like a refund please.**
Assistant: *I could lose my job if I do what you are asking.*
Customer: **I appreciate your worry about losing your job, but I would like a refund please.**
Assistant: *If you come back this afternoon the manager will be here.*
Customer: **I appreciate that you would like me to come back when the manager is here but it is not convenient. I would like a refund please.**
Assistant: *This is ridiculous, you sound like a broken record.*
Customer: **I realize that's how I must sound but I would like a refund please.**
Assistant: *OK, give me the shoes!*

Maybe this does strike you as rather ridiculous, but it works! I feel that it needs a bit of gall to do this but on certain occasions, when you have nothing to lose in terms of a relationship it is amazingly effective, as long as you are within your legal rights in your request. I don't advocate it in situations where you need to have an ongoing relationship with somebody as it can feel like aggression if you are on the receiving end. Your voice should maintain the same volume, tone and determination throughout – concentrating objectively on the outcome you want.

## ASSERTIVE CONTRACTING

So far we have dealt with spontaneous one-off situations. I would like to address the issues involved in longer-term contractual relationships. If somebody is going to supply a product or service to you in a customized way, where you become their 'client', then you deserve to remain as impressed with their performance or product throughout the contractual period, as you were when they were trying to sell themselves to you. Take the following examples: arranging a wedding reception, employing people to do building work, choosing a dentist, hairdresser, counsellor or GP – and similar situations where you are going to pay somebody to provide something which isn't readily visible. In business, the examples might include buying in consultancy, training, specialized technology and software. Off the shelf goods clearly outline the capacity and features of the product, but it is far more difficult purchasing specialist services. Computer software is a frequent example of this; companies contract software designers to produce certain outcomes for them but can hit problems when the software fails to meet the requirements of the business.

Any contractual relationship should begin by consciously going through the process of the contract and its delivery. For example: you are having an extension built on your home. Some of the things you might check out with the builder **before the work starts** are the following:

- What date do you expect the work to be finished?
- When do you intend to start?
- Where will your materials be stored?
- What are your working hours?
- What facilities do your workers require throughout the day?
- How many people are likely to be on site?
- Who is responsible for quality and how can they be contacted?
- What are the arrangements for payment – will you require any interim payment for materials etc.?

On commencement of the work, I suggest a discussion on how the workers will conduct themselves and what they can expect from you. For example:
- Precise instructions on what access they have to the house.
- The standard you expect the area to be left in at the end of each day.
- What you will or won't provide in terms of refreshment and toilet facilities.
- What they and you would like to be called.
- Information on pets or children which is helpful for them to know.
- An agreement that if there is a problem, on either side, it will be discussed.

By going through this process everybody knows exactly where they stand and you have set a customer/ provider relationship from the start. This might sound cold and humourless, but it doesn't have to be that way at all. If conducted with respect it is usually met with acceptance and a willingness to please. Of course, it is possible, even likely, that they will have something to say about you at their first tea break, but they are probably going to talk about you anyway. At least you will have a less painful few weeks ahead than if people take over your home and you feel too timid to stop them.

## Contracting personal services

A rather different example is when you are selecting somebody for a personal service – such as a counsellor, osteopath or acupuncturist. These are occasions when we can fall into the trap of being intimidated, both by the situation of vulnerability which brings us to the person and by their 'professional' status.

**Never forget that you have the right to NOT know something and you have the right to ask questions.**

Some of the following questions might be appropriate in seeking a helper whether it is a counsellor for a personal problem or an alternative medicine practitioner for a physical problem.

- What exactly happens in a 'session' with you?
- How often and for how long would you expect me to be coming to you?
- How much will it cost me? When do I pay? What happens if I have to cancel an appointment?
- What experience do you have of dealing with this type of problem?
- Do you have a particular approach?
- Would it be helpful if I read something about . . . (counselling/acupuncture/homeopathy)?
- Would you be willing for my partner to come along with me?

You may find that it is not necessary to ask any of these because the practitioner will go through this kind of information with you as a matter of course. However, giving some thought to what you want to know and preparing the questions will enable you to behave assertively and eliminate any feeling of intimidation you might have.

This is never so essential as when visiting a doctor. Like everything else in life, there are good and bad examples of GPs and consultants. Unfortunately it is often pot luck whether we are confronted with somebody who listens to us and offers clear information and explanation. For many people, going to see their doctor is an experience which makes them feel afraid and inadequate – add to this their concerns about what might be wrong with them and assertiveness can go right out of the window!

**Always prepare what you want to tell the doctor.**
Some people suggest writing it furtively on your hand, but I say write notes on a sheet of paper and take it out in front of the doctor. Let them see that you have a list of questions to ask. I know they are very, very busy people and they may be dealing with patients who are far sicker than you. But you have rights, we have a National Health Service which we pay for. The better the consultation, the less likely you are to waste the doctor's time further, by having to go back. Of course we don't have the right to waste a doctor's time. We should be aware of surgery times and not take advantage of the on-call system. But we should use it when essential. Remember, you own your body. It is your responsibility to look after it, but sometimes we need help and we have the right to ask for that help from a doctor. You are their customer – they wouldn't have a job if they didn't have any patients.

# CHAPTER 8 SUMMARY

- Be aware of consumer rights and seek accurate information.
- A smile and pleasant approach always helps.
- Don't moan; take positive action or put up with the situation – the choice is yours.
- Stay in control; don't be seduced by sales talk.
- Prepare before making a complaint.
- Avoid entering casually into contracts; take assertive action at the start.

# Saying 'no' and setting boundaries

*'I open my mouth to say NO and it comes out as NO PROBLEM!!'*

I haven't come across many people who don't occasionally find themselves saying 'Yes' when they really want to say 'No'. It's great when people are helpful and obliging towards one another, saying 'Yes' to a request and meaning it. But there is a price to pay for saying 'Yes' when we really mean 'No'. Apart from practical issues of time management or giving away things which belong to us, the big price of not saying 'No' is reduced self-esteem and feelings of anger and resentment.

There are situations when people make requests in a manipulative way so that saying 'No' is almost impossible. I recently ran the gauntlet of a line of tin-rattlers all asking me 'would you like to help disabled children?' What kind of monster does it make me if my answer to this question is a categoric 'NO!' In this case a qualified *'No, I already have a charity which I regularly support, thank you'* is the best answer.

Manipulation can appear in many forms and we must learn to recognize it in order that we remain in control rather than be controlled by a manipulative person.

Changing your mind is not giving in to manipulation so long as you are choosing. Remember – keeping hold of your own power and responding to people from within your own rights helps you to stay in control and make the right choices for you and for the situation.

Give some thought now to your own experiences – there may be some people to whom you find it particularly difficult to say 'No' whilst with others it is easy.

*Consider these examples:*
**Saying 'No' might be *easy with* . . .**

| PERSON | SITUATION |
|---|---|
| 1. Best friend | anything |
| 2. Strangers | charity box collections |
| 3. Sales people | doorstep double glazing sales |

**Saying 'No' might be *difficult with* . . .**

| PERSON | SITUATION |
|---|---|
| 1. Neighbour | borrowing garden tools |
| 2. Work colleague | collections for birthday presents |
| 3. Doorstep sales | unemployed young people selling dishcloths! |

*Compare these examples:*
Example 1 – A true 'best friend' will respect and accept you whatever you do; you don't need to demonstrate to them that you are generous or obliging. A neighbour might be somebody who doesn't really know you, but you would like to be on good terms with. It is a big risk to cause them to suspect you of meanness or pettiness. So, despite the fact that you always have to go round to 'borrow' your lawnmower back, or spend time cleaning the picnic box out before you can use it again, you find

yourself saying 'Yes' to their request when inside you can hear the screeching echo of 'No' reverberating through your body! This leaves you with negative feelings about the neighbour when in fact it is *you* who has allowed the situation to happen. Of course, some people will take advantage of us if we let them, but who is to blame? We can't control other people, but we can control ourselves.

Example 2 – It might be easy to say 'No' to a stranger who is collecting for a charity in which you have no particular interest, but fear of being talked about as 'mean' or 'antisocial' by work colleagues can lead you to donate money which you really can't afford, even though you hardly know the person whose birthday it is.

Example 3 – Saying 'No' to a professional salesperson who knocks on your door might be much easier than when it is somebody who you feel sorry for. In reality, both of those people probably need a 'sale' quite desperately, but you may be less likely to feel guilt saying 'No' to one than to the other.

Now give some thought to your own responses; it may be helpful to write them below.

Saying 'No' is *easy for me with* . . .

**PERSON**          **SITUATION**

1.

2.

3.

4.

5.

Saying 'No' is *difficult for me with* . . .

PERSON          SITUATION
1.
2.
3.
4.
5.

*Think through the differences in your two lists.*

–  Is the ability to say 'No' related to power?
–  Does it have something to do with guilt?
–  Are the relationships involved in your first list more
   secure?

*Go through your second list and in each case try to identify what the difficulty is with regard to saying 'No'.*

**How do I feel? What might happen if I say 'No'?**
1

2

3

4

5

Now that you have done this you can make decisions about whether **what might happen if you say 'No'** is acceptable to you or not. You may remember from previous chapters that playing the 'nice guy' can lead to all sorts of unhappy repercussions. On the other hand, this book has stressed the importance of choice in situations; you can **choose** to be assertive, but sometimes it might not be right for you, or for the situation.

## WHY IS SAYING NO SO DIFFICULT?

In any dialogue the response is generally much quicker when people say 'Yes' rather than 'No'. Take the opportunity to observe some conversations and you are likely to hear more words used when people are refusing than when they are accepting something. This is to do with part of the conventions of language – a 'politeness' which is normal in the usage of English. The word 'yes' is less frequently followed by qualification or explanation than the word 'no'. Try this out – ask people some questions and see what happens. I personally have found this reassuring; so often people are anxious about their inability to say 'no' and put themselves down for it. Realizing that there is a linguistic ritual to refusing requests can help you to learn the techniques involved in a less emotional and more mechanical way.

We are conditioned to consider other people; think about some of the parental messages which you identified in Chapter 6 – you were probably rewarded for 'doing as you're told' but reprimanded for refusing.

'Don't you say no to me' said in a harsh, authoritative tone, signifies a transitory withdrawal of love from the person who we most need to love us. Consequently, even as adults, the very idea of saying 'No' can subconsciously fill us with guilt, dread and foreboding. Remember, this isn't necessarily still relevant to you – the adult – who can rationally decide whether 'Yes' or 'No' is an appropriate response to a request from your boss, your neighbour, a member of your family, or somebody rattling a tin in the high street.

PLEASE CARRY OUT THE FOLLOWING
INSTRUCTIONS:
– PUT THIS BOOK DOWN

- LIFT YOUR CHIN
- SAY LOUDLY AND CLEARLY 'NO'

So often people say *'I just can't say "no".'* Well, you can – you just did. Don't forget that there is a difference between *can't* and *won't*. In one case we are in control and choosing, in the other we are suggesting that we are not in control and have no choice.

## HOW TO SAY 'NO'

**Remind yourself every now and then that . . .**
- You have the right to say 'no' without feeling guilty.
- It is OK for other people to say 'no' to you.
- Saying 'yes' when you mean 'no' may reduce your self-esteem.
- It is better to say 'no' at the time than to let somebody down later.
- Saying 'yes' to extra work or obligations might cause you stress.
- Taking on too much might lower your standard of work or mean that the important people in your life don't get their due attention.
- It might not be such a big deal for the other person to get a 'no' response.
- Being respected and respecting yourself is more important than being liked.

**The process . . .**
- As with other techniques of assertiveness, try it out in relatively uncomplicated situations – something impersonal or casual where you usually just drift into a 'yes'.
- If your immediate response is 'no', hang on to this

before being 'nice' takes over – remember what the cost of saying 'yes' might be.

- Be firm but polite – *I'm OK – You're OK*.
- Give a reason if you feel it's appropriate, but not an excuse – people can usually see through excuses and it can be insulting hearing that somebody doesn't respect you enough to be honest with you.
- Buy some thinking time – *I'll get back to you later . . . I need to check my diary*.
- Ask for more information – *how long will it take? . . . when will I get back? . . . is there anybody else who could do this for you?* These are also tactics for giving yourself thinking time.
- Use body language and your voice – to show that by saying 'no' you are not being hostile; to demonstrate that you mean what you say and are not going to be manipulated.
- Stay calm and relaxed – drop your shoulders and breathe deeply so that your voice and pace remains assertive, not aggressive or passive.
- Think it through – by listening to the other person you might realize that actually you want to say 'yes' after all. Don't be manipulated but it is perfectly all right to change your mind if you are doing so out of choice.

*Like most things, with practice saying 'NO' becomes easier. You have got choice but first you must choose whether you want to be choosing!*

## SETTING BOUNDARIES

Often situations are not so cut and dried as merely demanding a straight 'yes' or 'no' answer. Imagine that some old friends have telephoned you to say that they intend to visit you over a bank holiday weekend. Last time they stayed with you, you felt that they were around for too long, but you really like these people and would love to spend *some* of the weekend with them.

**Which of the answers below are you likely to give?**

1. *'Yes, great, we'd love to see you.'*
   Then put the phone down and increasingly regret the fact that you have to give a whole weekend over to them. So much so, in fact, that thoughts of your friends bring resentment and tension rather than pleasure.
2. *'Oh, what a shame, we'd love to see you but we've already arranged to go away that weekend.'*
   Then spend the weekend worrying every time the phone rings, that they might 'catch you out'.
3. *'Well actually, we're going to be doing things in the house so we're not available.'*
   Then feel guilty and also regret not having some time with your friends.

**The other option is to state your boundaries clearly.**
   The reply might go something like this:
   *'It will be nice to see you but we have got a few things we want to do that weekend. How about coming here on Sunday lunchtime and staying until Monday afternoon?'*
   You have made it clear what you do and don't want, and your friends know where they stand. They can then choose to accept or reject your offer. If they do re-state that they want to come for the whole weekend then you can use the *broken record* technique to repeat what you would like:
   *'We really would like you to come. We've got a few other things we want to do, so seeing you from Sunday to Monday would be great.'*

By repeating yourself, using the *broken record* technique, you reinforce what you do want and make that message clear.

Make sure that your head is full of positive thinking whilst this is going on. Ask yourself:

– Whose home is it? (*yours of course*)
– Whose time is it? (*yours of course*)
– Do I have the right to be respected for what I do or don't want? (*I hope, by now, that I don't have to prompt you into a loud 'YES'*)

When your friends do arrive, you are likely to be pleased to see them and delighted to devote your time to their stay. My experience of this has always been that it has strengthened relationships as people have greater mutual respect and trust when they know where they stand with one another.

**Setting clear boundaries will give people an understanding of what is or isn't acceptable to you. When people overstep your boundaries it can make you feel used or abused.**

Examples of overstepping boundaries:

• Taking advantage of your generosity
• Using language or making jokes which are offensive to you
• Touching you or encroaching on your physical space
• Outstaying a welcome

You may be able to think of situations where something has 'gone too far' and you have felt angry, upset or uncomfortable about it.

I was reminded of the importance of boundaries

when, at a large company function the guest speaker, a famous comedian, made references about people in the audience. There was a discomfort amongst many of his audience who felt that he had 'overstepped the mark'. Some people dismissed this displeasure as sour grapes or lack of a sense of humour, but I felt that it was quite right to feel upset by a situation where cheap laughs were gained by an expensive comedian.

**It is important to respect other people's boundaries. If you are not sure what they are, then find out. Ask them what it is they would like from you and how they want to be treated.**

When people have suffered bereavement or sadness in their life they often find themselves being avoided, as if they were contagious. The explanation is usually that 'you don't know what to say, do you?'

My answer to this is to ask them whether they want to talk about it? How would they like you to treat them? Is it better if you do or don't mention the person they have lost? By doing this you give the grieving person the opportunity to state his boundaries and you are able to behave in a way that respects those boundaries without the person feeling isolated.

Think about different aspects and relationships in your life.

What are your boundaries – what do you choose to protect?

**Example**

| SITUATION/ RELATIONSHIP | BOUNDARIES |
| --- | --- |
| Work | Willing to give all when I'm there but not to take work home or stay after 6 p.m. unless very special circumstances. |

| Home | Want a reasonable standard of tidiness and order in the house. |
| Friends | Will give help but not expect to be 'dumped' on. |

Other examples of BOUNDARIES might include possessions, time, family, hobbies, sex, children, children's friends, neighbours, privacy, religion, work relationships . . .

*Now write your examples here:*

SITUATION/         BOUNDARIES
RELATIONSHIP

# CHAPTER 9 SUMMARY

- Accept that saying 'No' is difficult, but not usually as difficult as the consequences of saying 'Yes' when you don't really want to.
- Remember that you have the right to refuse and that other people can refuse your requests.
- Don't use *I can't*, it is more empowering to say *I won't* or *I don't want to*.
- Know what your boundaries are – express them when appropriate and be prepared to respect other people's boundaries.

# CHAPTER 10

# Positive constructive communication

It will have become increasingly clear to you how important communication is to successful assertiveness. One thing that defines us as humans is our ability to communicate. As we grow and develop, so do our communication skills. This chapter deals mainly with communication at work but the principles and techniques will be equally effective when you apply them in every day life.

Poor communication skills always emerge as one of the main concerns of employers in recruiting good people. After Technical/Practical requirements, the two most sought after skills are Communication and Customer Handling. This applies at all levels, in all industries and organizations. Maybe you have tried getting information from somebody who is technically brilliant but can't actually communicate at a level that will achieve everybody's needs. Similarly, however creative somebody is, if they are not able to translate their ideas into workable solutions and saleable products then they will fail. It is taken for granted that communication is 'common sense'. Well, maybe, but my view then is that common sense is not very common. Besides, my 'common sense', gleaned from my Parent ego state, might fundamentally differ from yours. When people are new to a job, a team, an organization, a group, it is assertive to initiate them in 'how we do things here' rather than getting frustrated because they do it their way, which is seen as wrong. This initiation should include basic guidelines on style, standards, and channels of communication.

## COMMUNICATION IS COMPLEX

In every dialogue between you and me there is:
*The person who I think I am*
*The person who you think I am*
*The person who I think you think I am*
*The person who you think I think you are . . .*

Okay, I'll stop there!

But just consider how little notice you take of somebody who you regard as insignificant, compared to somebody who you see as powerful? On the other hand, how effective are you in communicating with somebody who you think is not impressed by or interested in what you have to say?

In Chapter 1 we looked at the **Five Basic Principles of Assertive Communication**. Remember?

**Direct      Appropriate      Responsible**

**Calm      Listening**

Let's look now at other fundamental elements.

## SENDER – RECEIVER

When we need to get a message across it is our responsibility not only to take control of what we send, but also to consider how it will be received. We can do this by eliminating *interference*.

Stop now and take a moment to give some thought to what interferes with messages that you send or receive.

Maybe some of the ideas you have come up with are about clarity of words, using the appropriate medium, time and place, body language, and, once you really start to think about it, a whole lot more.

## EIGHT STEPS TO CLEAR COMMUNICATION

- Know what you want to achieve/what your objective is
- Choose the appropriate method – face-to-face, telephone, letter, e-mail, words, pictures. Which will best achieve your objective?
- Choose the time and place
- Gain attention
- Establish and maintain an open relationship – *I'm OK You're OK*
- Actively listen and appreciate the listener/receiver's interests
- Be clear, brief, coherent
- Control your non-verbal messages and read those of your receiver/s

Is this a checklist that you are in the habit of using? Or do you, like most of us on most days, just open your mouth, or the phone line or the outbox and *send*.

## To text or not to text – the pros and perils of immediacy

Research tells us that men now express their love in words far more than before. The medium? Text messaging. This is great and I'm all for it. But the down side of this ingenious technology is that people are able to, and do, send messages that they perhaps wouldn't express if they waited until the morning, or until the emotion of a situation had subsided. Before sending off your message check with yourself: would I say this to the person if they were standing in front of me?

## Email Etiquette

Bear in mind that when your message appears in somebody's Inbox it may be far lower on their priority list than it is on yours. In this case, it might not be the most effective method of communicating if it is an urgent matter for you.

How do your e-mails look to the receiver? I am amazed at the number of people who would never send out a letter or report which wasn't accurate in spelling and grammar, yet their e-mails are full of errors. This serves to undermine the message and therefore will *interfere* with the objective.

Just a word about CAPITAL LETTERS. They are the visual equivalent of shouting and as we have seen in earlier chapters, nobody really responds well to being shouted at.

# BLAME IT ON COMMUNICATION

'The problem in this place is lack of communication.' I would be a rich woman if I had collected money every time I heard somebody say that. Have you ever said it?

If so, what did you really mean? You weren't being told enough? The grapevine was stronger than formal channels of communication? Or maybe you just weren't being told what you wanted to hear?

My first response to this is always 'what do you want to know and what is the best way of trying to find out?'

## HIDING PLACES

In work and personal situations people complaining about lack of communication can be one of those 'hiding places' that people use as an excuse for not dealing assertively with an issue. You can recognize these hiding places by the use of abstract words: *management* never trust us; *relationships* have been soured; *the company* keep us in the dark; *communication* has broken down. Another way of recognizing hiding places is by use of absolute terms: *nobody* listens to me; I *always* get blamed. You probably have your own examples and can start to recognize that there is an element of 'victim' in all this where the person opts out of taking responsibility because things are 'being done to them'.

## SENDING POWERFUL MESSAGES

I am not saying that the issue that people are concerned about when they use such terms has no importance, of course it has. What I am saying is that when we use vague, unclear messages we give people the opportunity to dismiss what we are saying and ignore our grumbles. If you recognize that you sometimes are a **sender** of indirect language then I suggest you refer back within this chapter, to the 5 principles of assertive communication, use the 8 steps in order to express your concerns assertively and see how much more powerfully it will be received.

## CLARIFYING THE MESSAGE

If you are on the **receiver** end of indirect messages then you can use assertive communication skills to discover what somebody really means. The skill here is in effective questioning. What we need to do is **probe** in order to glean more information, not aggressively question in a way that will put the person on the defensive.

References to *'management'* should be clarified: *'who exactly do you mean?'* if you are a brave manager you might ask *'do you mean me?'* When somebody tells us that *'communication has broken down'* we need to ask what they want to know about. If we don't ask these questions we miss opportunities. We fail to find out what is going on in somebody's head that may be getting in the way of their motivation or self-esteem, or that they are using it as an excuse to be negative. Similarly, words like *'nobody'* and *'always'* can be probed: *'who exactly?' 'Can you give me an example?'*

A word of caution here: what you have just read is in itself a useful example of the difficulty of communication. Just reading the words off the page will not necessarily equip you with good advice. Take the question 'who exactly do you mean?' and say it out loud in a variety of ways. You will hear that it can sound aggressive, defensive, sarcastic, gossipy. The intonation you use will affect the response you get. When we probe, we stay with the words and ideas that somebody expresses and help them to extend them. 'How do you mean?' 'In what way?' 'Can you think of an example?' These terms, used in an 'I'm OK, You're OK' tone of voice will gain trust and open up dialogue.

## IT'S THE WAY THAT HE SAID IT!

I'm sure you can relate to a time when you have been upset, angered or confused by **how** something has been said to you rather than **what** has been said. In many of the examples in this book you may have felt strong disagreement with what I have proposed as 'model' statements. Yes, I understand that completely because you are not able to hear my tone of voice as I would actually speak them.

Research tells us that the effectiveness of communication relies 7 per cent on words, 35 per cent on tone of voice and 58 per cent on body language. The statistics relate to face-to-face communication but are still relevant to other media even though the numbers may change. Think about receiving a letter: the envelope it arrives in, the quality of the paper, the layout, the importance of the signature, will precede the actual content in influencing your initial impression and consequently the letter's effectiveness in achieving its objective. These judgements are likely to be subconscious, we will not be aware of making them. So, that was just a letter. Imagine how much more complex our subconscious responses are to flesh and blood. Except of course it rarely is flesh and blood, unless you work in a casualty ward or a massage parlour.

## WHAT ARE YOU SAYING WHEN YOU ARE NOT SAYING ANYTHING?

Facial expression, posture, grooming, eye contact, proximity and a whole lot more communicate to us before somebody has spoken a word. When I facilitate discussions on body language some people are antagonistic to the ideas because they have a strong sense that '*you should take people as they are and not make judgements*'. Well, yes, I am in agreement with this, but the reality is that we don't know *what* people are, we can only take them *as we perceive them to be*. If somebody is smiling, with a relaxed, confident posture, is appropriately clean with an inoffensive odour, makes comfortable eye contact and is standing or sitting at the right distance from me, then I am likely to subconsciously feel at ease and happy to listen to what they have to say. If, however, the opposite is true in one or two points, then my subconscious 'judgement' will be affecting how I receive what they have to say. The effect of my judgement in this case is likely to trigger a negative response towards the person and therefore obscure whatever they proceed to communicate. They will not necessarily get their point across as **they** think or feel because I will have interpreted it as **I** perceive them.

So what can we do about this? Once again, two perspectives: sender and receiver.

### On the receiving end

Be aware of the dangers of making judgements about people. Our judgements block us in. We deny ourselves the opportunity of experiencing people who are different from us. The list of features of body language that affect communication intentionally omits factors such as age, colour, clothes, size, gender, ability/disability. These represent overt prejudices but of course will be highly influential in the way we receive communication. Again, I urge you to be aware of these prejudices, to exit the **Parent Ego State** where these prejudices are stored and try to receive the communication in your **adult state.**

## Sending Messages

The sender has the opportunity to ask 'what do I want this person/these people to see when I communicate my message?' If the answer is an **assertive** communicator then it is up to you to ensure that is what they will be looking at.

**Facial expression** should be appropriate to the subject. A smile is winning, disarming and can put people at ease, but empathy with the situation, the subject and the receiver will help you to determine when it is appropriate. I have witnessed people trying to deliver good customer service and being told 'you can wipe that grin off your face' by their customer! Similarly, if you are delivering bad news then your message might not be properly understood if you are saying it with a smile.

**Posture** will communicate confidence, energy and personal control if you get it right. As we have seen in earlier chapters, head up with relaxed shoulders and an open stance will demonstrate a command of yourself and the situation.

**Grooming and general appearance** work in a number of ways. Personal hygiene is fundamental; we can't wait to get away from people who don't smell very nice, however convincing their spoken message may be. Appearance in general is another one of those thorny issues that people argue about. Personally, I advocate a dress code in the workplace. It eliminates inappropriate dress and establishes a corporate, business-like ethos internally and externally. This can be interpreted in a way that is appropriate to the industry or organization's aims. People argue that it goes against individuality and people's rights. I see their point but this is another issue

116

where common sense isn't necessarily common and I've observed many situations where inappropriate dress in the workplace has got in the way of assertiveness because the 'sender' has not been taken seriously by the 'receiver'.

Another important aspect of appearance is looking organized, whether it's your desk, your bag, your papers: anything that can be seen by the receiver will have an influence on the effectiveness of your communication.

Comfortable **eye contact** demonstrates respect and straightforwardness. When we describe somebody as 'a bit shifty' it is usually because they have avoided our eye. On the other hand, a stare can feel very aggressive. If you find it difficult to make eye contact with somebody try focussing on the bridge of their nose. After a while, if you are communicating well and listening genuinely you will forget about it and eye contact will become easy and natural. When people are thinking and remembering things, they will look away from you before they make a response. This is normal and natural, not an avoidance of eye contact.

Your **proximity** to another person will have an effect on how they receive your communication. If you step into somebody's space they may feel threatened by you and see it as aggressive. The response may then be that they become aggressive or that they back off passively. **Assertive communicators** want to maintain an assertive dialogue so it is important to be sensitive to other people's space. The cultural norm for Northern Europeans is just short of arm's length. If you look around, you will see that most business or formal communication is conducted at this distance. Be aware though that this isn't necessarily the cultural norm for everybody. In many cultures people are comfortable being a lot closer. They are not being offensive, this is merely a different norm. If you feel uncomfortable then step back a little, maintaining eye contact and a positive regard toward that person.

*Just a word about situations of potential danger. If you are in doubt about a person, with regard to your personal safety, then there is no doubt. Protect yourself by removing yourself from the situation. This book is about Assertiveness. It will help you to deal effectively with difficult people and difficult situations. However, if you are in a role that involves potentially dangerous interaction with the public then you have the right to be given clear guidelines and good training by your employer.*

## INFLUENCING SKILLS

In order to influence we need to have power. Your reaction may be that this counts you out if you don't see yourself in a position of power, but it doesn't necessarily mean high status, social or business 'muscle'. There are many sources of power and they change in different situations. Think of an office junior working in a place where a computer system has recently been introduced. That young person may have far better IT skills than his or her colleagues just because they have worked with them all through school and college. This gives them an opportunity to assert themselves and have influence in that situation. Another example is somebody who, regardless of their status, has really good interpersonal skills. People will listen to this person and be influenced by what they have to say.

Conventional status is an obvious form of power.

The hirer and firer in an organization, holds authority, but not necessarily the *influence* that motivates people to do a good job, take pride in their work and continually seek to improve. Influencing is far more subtle than wielding power. It is about *persuading* people to your point of view in order that they act or respond in the way you want them to. I choose persuading rather than advising. I have come to the conclusion that unsolicited advice wastes valuable breath. If it worked then none of us would ever be overweight, unfit, hungover or guilty of speeding. There is advice coming at us all the time, but we are not necessarily influenced by it.

## ASSERTIVE INFLUENCING

This is another instance when a win-win outcome will achieve the best goal. Effective influencing requires a respect for the person/people who we want to influence, not manipulation.

**Effective questioning will involve people in the issue.** We often assume that others are motivated by the same things we are motivated by. This isn't true, so therefore they will not necessarily be influenced by the same things we are. When we influence people successfully it is because we have convinced them of the **benefits** of doing something. Discovering what is important to somebody, what their values are, what motivates them, helps us to plan how best we can influence them.

I have recently been working with an organization undergoing a lot of change: nothing new there of course. But what was refreshing was the ease with which the change evolved. The company spent a lot of time understanding the values of its employees; what was important to them in their jobs and therefore what motivated them. As you would expect, salary was high on the list but so was pride in the product, teamwork and opportunities to be creative. With this understanding, the company was able to introduce change in a way that was acceptable to people because they were able to see the benefit of it.

## THE POWER OF LISTENING

The example I have just given can only happen if people have developed their skills in listening. As we have seen throughout this book, listening is essential to assertiveness. In his excellent book *Seven Skills of Highly Effective People*, Peter Covey uses the phrase *seek first to understand, then to be understood*. This is the opposite to how we usually do things. It is more common to take the 'what you need to understand . . .' approach. We try to implant what we want somebody to know without first hearing their perspective. By listening to somebody, you can learn what they actually think, feel, want, i.e. what is of value to them. This then gives the opportunity to express what you want in terms that will be acceptable to them.

There used to be a billboard advertizement for a charity concerned with children. It was a picture of a scruffy, spotty, unsmiling teenage boy. The caption said 'what he needs is a damned good listening to'. I still find this very powerful as a reminder that if we want somebody to behave differently then the starting point is to find out why they behave like they do. This is very relevant to managing people, bringing up children and enjoying healthy personal relationships.

## YOU JUST DON'T LISTEN

In reality not listening is more complicated than 'just' not doing it. As the questionnaire on Listening in Chapter 1 of this book demonstrates: what actually happens is that we think we are listening but more often than not we are listening to what we think we are hearing rather than what is being said. People whose profession is to listen have spent years being trained to do so. It is a very difficult skill to achieve mastery in. In a recorded counselling or therapy situation it is likely that the voice of the listener will only be heard for 10 per cent of the fifty minutes. The benefit to people of being able to *just talk* can be amazing. On the other hand, if you tape normal, everyday conversation you will hear a 'my go' – 'your go' pattern. It might be something like this. 'Did you have a good weekend?' 'Yeah it was great we went down to the coast, it was a lovely day.' 'Oh we just stayed home and did the garden.' Normal, natural and perfectly acceptable. But can you see that there is no real listening here? A real listening response to 'we went down to the coast, it was a lovely day' would be 'that sounds nice. Where did you go/what did you do?' Real listening doesn't involve capturing the subject and making it your own, it involves enabling the other person to continue in order that they can express more. **A warning:** I am not suggesting that we should pursue 'real' listening all the time. We would never get through the day. The conversation I illustrated is normal social interaction. What I am drawing attention to is that when we need to assert ourselves it is necessary to **really listen** in order to maximize our understanding and make the appropriate response. Apart from Assertiveness Training, I would say that the workshop I run that empowers people most is that on Listening. By really listening to what is said, we can understand and gain control of a situation.

## POWERFUL LANGUAGE

I was recently asked to put together a phrase book of assertive responses. Here are a few examples from it but I would like to urge you to do this for yourself. Some examples would be:

*No, I won't come with you at lunchtime, thanks.*
Rather than *I can't.*

*That's a good idea and we can develop it, but this time we will do it this way.*
Rather than No, *that won't work, we'll do it like this.*

*I don't know where I want to go to eat.*
Rather than *I don't mind [and then rejecting every suggestion!].*

*Sounds great, thank you for asking me, but not this time.*

*It's not possible for me to do that by this afternoon but I can do . . .*

*Tell me what you would have liked me to do in that situation?*

Now some of yours. Standard responses to situations in which you want to behave more assertively:

Once again, remember that the impact of your words will depend on your tone of voice and what you are expressing with your body.

## CHAPTER 10 SUMMARY

- Communication is complex. We need to think through our objective and plan accordingly
- Tone of voice and body language are far more powerful than words
- Good listening enables you to understand and consequently to know how to influence somebody
- Use language that shows that you are strong and in control

# CHAPTER 11

# Harmonious discipline

Throughout this book I have been encouraging you to treat yourself well, to think kindly of yourself and to eliminate destructive, self-critical messages that play in your head. You need to be the best friend you can possibly be to yourself in order that your self-esteem is good and you can be truly assertive. I hope however, that you have learned that all this doesn't come without effort. Meeting deadlines, achieving goals, getting fit, losing weight and becoming assertive all come into the category of 'no pain, no gain'. Just keep remembering though *if you do what you always do, you'll get what you always get*. If you would like different outcomes, then do yourself the kindness of changing. Assert self-discipline.

The word 'discipline' conjures up different things for different people. (I am aware that for some it will evoke an image of Ms Whiplash in all her gear! Fun though it might be to link assertiveness with this, I will maintain discipline and the approval of my publisher by leaving that subject to somebody better qualified.)

Generally we associate discipline with order and control, but I fear that it also has a tinge of restraint, punishment and repression about it, which doesn't necessarily fit the 'have it all' society which we have grown to expect. I suppose it's not much fun.

In this chapter I will talk about three aspects of this rather unfashionable notion and demonstrate that life isn't really much 'fun' without an appropriate amount of discipline, specifically:

**Self-discipline, Workplace Discipline
and Parental Discipline.**

## ACHIEVING BALANCE

In our society of affluence and relative ease, one of the challenges is achieving and maintaining balance in our lives. Too much leisure can lead to boredom, too little makes Jack a dull girl/boy. We read lottery winners' stories demonstrating that too much money can unbalance life and lead to unhappiness. Within a morning, you can feel like you have too much time on your hands and then panic that you will fail to meet a deadline or to arrive somewhere on time. Discipline too requires an appropriate balance: whether it is with yourself, your kids, your employees or your hobby. Too little and you will not achieve what you want, too much and you create a regime which is harsh and inhibiting rather than creative and relaxed.

### Positive Stress
An interesting, happy life will have an appropriate amount of stress to keep us motivated, challenged, interested and interesting. Lack of stimulation and challenge can lead to 'rust out'; a form of stress where the lack of demands may lead to boredom, depression and low self-esteem. On the other hand, when work or life in general

becomes too challenging and we cannot see a successful resolution of these challenges we suffer a 'burn out' stress. At its worst this leads to serious physical or mental illness but even in a mild form it can be extremely debilitating. Once we get out of balance we start to make mistakes, forget things, lose sight of priorities and feel bad about ourselves.

Assertiveness comes into play in controlling stress like so many other areas. I am frequently contracted to work with individuals who are suffering ill effects of workplace stress and whilst every situation and every individual is different, a common element is lack of assertiveness. This happens **outwardly**, by an inability to say 'no' to people and therefore taking on far more than is realistic and **inwardly**, by not having the confidence to assert influence. What happens to people in these situations is that they have become out of balance. Work has spilled over into personal time, through putting in extra hours or waking in the night worrying about it, often both. Consequently the essential, healthy balance between work and family/social life is disturbed.

### It's Polite to Wait to Be Asked

### Or

### If You Don't Ask You Don't Get

Which of the above **parent ego** messages is more familiar to you? Being **assertive** involves not waiting to be asked, but taking the initiative and going for it. Never impolitely of course, but certainly with an eye on what you want to achieve and putting the necessary work into action. How often have you said you'd really like to do something but then found an excuse for putting it off?

Using the weather, finances, the dark nights, your boss, somebody's attitude – I've no doubt you can add other excuses of your own. Ask yourself this: *am I the sort of person who does things or the sort of person who talks about doing things?* If there is something you want, set your sights, assert some self-discipline and do it.

**Exercise.**
*Visualize yourself five years from now. Write down or mentally note the date. Now think about what you would like to be saying on that date about the previous five years of your life. That's it, from now until then. How would you like it to have been? Well: right **now** is the beginning of those five years and you have a lot of power to influence how they go. On whatever date it is you have written down you will have no power at all to influence what has passed. At the moment you have loads of power. Use it. Assert yourself.*

**Self-discipline is essential in achieving goals.** Getting the right balance will enable us to assert and maintain a level of self-discipline, which helps us to achieve our potential and at the same time allow us to feel happy about ourselves.

- Know what you want
- Set a plan
- Assess and develop the necessary skills
- Do the work
- Monitor your progress
- Adjust where necessary
- Recognize and celebrate achievement

This will work best if it really is **your** goal, compatible with your values and beliefs, and if the outcome is really what you want. We rarely achieve important goals because it is what somebody else wants for us. Whether it is a work or a personal issue, you need to be motivated, you have got to personally want to achieve the goal. Stop reading for a few moments and write down some things that you *should* or *have got to* do.

How does what you have written make you feel?

Now list things which you *want* to do.

Do you feel differently about these?

It is likely that you feel lighter, more positive, more motivated to do the second list and that you will succeed. Sadly, few of us can go through life only doing what we want so we have to find a way of motivating ourselves.

When you need to tackle something that you would prefer not to. Do you . . .

**Put it off by displacement activity?**
Suddenly tidying your Inbox, grooming the cat, checking up on an invoice or transferring information into your new diary all seem of greater priority. (I'm sure you have procrastinators of your own to add to these.)

**Exaggerate how bad it will be?**
Talking yourself into a scenario where failure is inevitable.

**Do the easy bits first?**
Then become more negative about it because it is now even less appealing.

**Wish the problem didn't exist?**
And consequently focus on the negative to make it even bigger.

Just writing this has plunged my brain into negative depths and so everything seems more difficult.

OK. Let's have a change of mind.

**Exercise.**
*Read this paragraph and then put the book down, lift your head up and put your shoulders back. Now take a deep breath and breathe out slowly, as you do so, relax any tension you are feeling. Take another deep breath and hold a positive image or word in your mind as you breathe away tension. Continue breathing well, focussing on the in breath, as it is this one which gives us energy. Hold your head up, maintain that positive thought or image, allow yourself a smile.*

Changing body posture to a positive pose has a powerful effect on the mind. In this alert but relaxed frame of body and mind I suggest you return to one of the items which you wrote under the *have got to do* heading.

Take an important one and firstly think about what the benefits will be of finishing this task. Visualize what it will look or how it will be when it is done. Keep visualizing this and focus on how you will feel having achieved it. Now set a plan: where, when, who, how. And ask yourself the following questions.

What could I do to make this less difficult or tedious? Be creative, maybe there is a different way of doing it.

What will my internal dialogue be as I am doing the task? Make this positive, encouraging and self-affirming.

How will I reward myself when it is completed? Make this relevant to the task. A really big one might deserve a weekend away. A smaller task might just earn you a glass of wine in the bath or a pint with a friend. Try to be creative about this; thinking about the reward at the end is a great motivator.

What will help me to remain positive and focused? Maintain a relaxed body posture. If possible ensure that the ambience around you is pleasant and that you have fresh air and light. I find music really helpful but that will depend upon the setting and the people around you.

If there is somebody who you admire who appears to achieve a lot whilst maintaining a happy, relaxed, balanced life, ask them how they assert self-discipline.

## DISCIPLINE AT WORK

If you are employed to manage, lead or supervize people then you have the responsibility to do so assertively. I was recently involved in a situation where the relationships in an office had become so dysfunctional that they were posing a threat to the business. Gary came into the department as Manager two years ago. A creative, brilliant marketeer with an easy going and friendly personality. Most people in the team were committed and motivated but there was one person whose personal life was always more important than her job. She started to take advantage of Gary's lack of supervision and got away with a lot, including taking extra holiday days which she was not recording and he didn't check. As you can imagine, other people in the team were pretty fed up with their colleague but also frustrated with Gary for allowing it to happen. His response was that he was busy dealing with important things and needed to be able to trust people to do the right thing.

Imagine a scale of management style with **PARTIC-IPATIVE** at one end and **AUTHORITARIAN** at the other. Most people, when asked, say that they prefer to be at the participative end; involving people in decisions, trusting them to perform well. When I then ask where **their** manager is on the scale they usually respond that their manager is further towards the authoritarian end. The discussion will usually take the direction of accepting that authoritarian is effective but as long as it is done '*nicely*'. What people are really meaning is that it is right that people with authority use that authority so long as their behaviour is **assertive: consistent, fair, honest and respectful.**

The result of the situation in Gary's case was that his passiveness tipped the balance of power. When he realized this he became extremely agitated and there was a public showdown. It took outside help to get people back working effectively together and the cost to the business was high. It would not have happened if Gary had laid down the rules, a notion which is unpalatable to people who claim to dislike an authoritarian approach to managing people.

### Why have rules?
Clear rules benefit both employers and employees. They set standards of conduct at work and make clear

to people what is expected of them. A disciplinary procedure is not about sacking people. It is a way of professionally ensuring that standards of conduct and performance are met. On occasions, situations of gross misconduct will lead to warnings or instant dismissal but mostly the situation of discipline is not over a dramatic incident. It is more like Gary's situation where there was a need for behaviour to be 'nipped in the bud'. Unfortunately though, many managers, like Gary, shy away from this and once the bud has bloomed it is far more difficult to deal with discretely and constructively.

**Discipline at work will be effective if we:**
- Make sure people know what the rules are
- Refer to the rules whenever necessary
- Negotiate changes to rules where appropriate
- Apply the discipline regime consistently and fairly

Are you familiar with your company's Disciplinary Procedure? I am frequently surprised how few managers answer *yes* to this question. It is likely that people in your HR department have spent a lot of time and money putting together your company's procedure. Locate it, read it, use it and ask for help in interpreting it. In the majority of cases you will not need to take formal action. Assertive discussions with your staff can ensure discipline is maintained and encourage self-discipline in them.

ACAS (Advisory, Conciliation and Arbitration Service) publish an excellent handbook on Discipline at Work. It will be useful to you whatever the size of your organization.

## PERFECT PARENTING

Congratulations to all of you who have been fortunate in having experienced such luxury as perfect parenting. On the other hand, if your parents were less than perfect in their treatment of you, I hope that books like this one can help you to gain and retain the self-esteem that you deserve.

Most of us are able to say that we had *good enough parenting*. That our parents did the best they could at the time and helped us to become OK adults. In Chapter 6 we focused on the influence of parenting from the child's point of view; now I would like to address how to get the balance right in asserting discipline with our own children.

**Free spirits.** You may be familiar with the view of the child as *tabula rasa*, a clean slate of purity upon which life's experiences writes an impression. It is a romantic notion and I like to fantasize that in a world of green pastures and sunshine a child can run free, experience nature and humanity and learn and grow within a bubble of protection and innocence.

It's not like that though is it?

We have to get to nursery, we have to watch the road, we have to negotiate the supermarket trolley, we have to do swimming lessons, and we have to sit tests at school. By the age of 7, children have learned that there are a great number of activities to get through each week. Not much running around fields barefoot is there? This is life as we live it and children need a framework of discipline in order to be happy and successful as a child, as an adolescent and as an adult. This is where the responsibility to assert a balanced discipline is at its most crucial. If you choose not to have self-discipline you are the real loser, if you don't assert discipline at work then your career and/or business will suffer. But if you fail to create and maintain appropriate discipline with children then you are seriously limiting the potential for your child to have a happy and fulfilling life. Yes, love and nurture their free spirit, give them space to experience and experiment, but do it in a framework of rules and boundaries inside which they feel secure.

**Kids Go Free!** It's great to see young children running in a park, playful and carefree. It is, however irritating to see and hear them running riot in a restaurant or public place. I can cite two recent experiences where people were becoming very agitated with children who were behaving inappropriately: one was in a church, the other in a hospital. Both of them places with a lot of space and in each case the children were all aged 6 and under. They were rushing around noisily in just the same way as they would behave in a play area. To some people the behaviour was irritating, to others disturbing and to a few, distressing. It was not the children's fault but it was the children who blame was projected on to. **We are not born knowing how to behave in different settings; we have the right to be taught this by our parents.** The notion of *citizenship* is now promoted in schools. Great idea, but I would hope that it is an extension of what people have been taught in the home: *that we have a responsibility to behave courteously towards other people with whom we share our world.*

Asserting discipline in a healthy, nurturing way involves telling the child what is and what is not acceptable behaviour rather than criticizing them in a **parent ego state** way which can lead them to adopt an *I'm not*

*OK* self-image. When reprimanding a child, try to direct your criticism to their behaviour, not to their whole self. You are showing them that you don't like what they are doing, not that you don't like them.

Have you heard children when playing together, say 'we're not allowed' in a perfectly neutral way? This suggests that they have been told a certain rule, accepted it and have due regard for that rule. When you hear your children saying this, congratulate yourself. You've done well.

I believe that confidence is at the core of good parenting just like in other forms of assertiveness. Your child loves you. They also trust you. They trust you to take care of them and therefore to know what is best. Yes of course, they will, from a very early age test that out, trying to assert their own way, but please don't forget that you are in charge. They have to wait their turn to be the grown up and they will only be able to become an effective adult if you have given them some boundaries as a child. Yes, discuss things; listen to their point of view, but in the end you are the one who must have the confidence to make decisions, to say 'no', to punish if the child has gone over the boundaries. I think a popular term for this is *tough love*.

**Saying what you mean, meaning what you say.** This is one of the basic principles of assertive communication and essential to setting clear boundaries. If you are going to make a threat to a child then you must carry it through. There is no use saying 'do that once more and I'll send you to bed' if you don't carry it through. (I personally think bed is a place which should be pleasurable to a child, not an implement of punishment. It's a place that we want them to enjoy being in so that they can charge their batteries and we can charge our own. Somewhere more neutral like the bottom stair can be more effective.) Maybe it is useful to prepare a short list of 'sanctions' to use, which are realistic and relevant. This is helpful because we can find ourselves having to back out of threats if they are unrealistic. For example 'you won't be allowed to play with Robin' isn't helpful if Robin's mother is just about to drop him off for the morning. Make sure you follow through the threat. Let the child know that the choice is with them: they can continue the behaviour but pay the penalty or change their behaviour.

As children grow the boundaries change. Decisions about how much freedom to allow them become more complex. There is a need for discussion in which both parties, parents and children/young people are thinking and communicating in their **adult ego state.** It's perfectly reasonable not to know the answer. A continuous phrase I have used with my children has been 'you didn't come with an instruction leaflet. I'm not sure what the best way is here, let's talk it through.' Involving a child in the decision making will give him/her tools with which to work things out and assert self-discipline throughout life. Of course, there will be times when you have to just come down on one side of a decision and hope it's right. It may not be the popular decision but you have the ultimate responsibility.

**Going it alone.** Parenting is a joyful experience despite the challenges and occasional heartache. I personally think that it is a two-person job so long as both people share an attitude and approach which the child sees as consistent. Parenting partners can share the highs and the lows together.

If, for whatever reason you are parenting alone then be kind to yourself. There is an enormous amount of giving in bringing up a child, make sure that you are also receiving the nourishment required for the job. In workplace situations I often advise people to seek out a **mentor.** Somebody who he or she respects and who they can use as a sounding board. I suggest something similar when you are parenting. Choose somebody who has experience of being a parent but whose children are at different ages and stages from yours. This person can be invaluable in giving you the encouragement and reassurance that is so essential to effective parenting.

Everything this book has covered about assertiveness and communication applies to our relationship with children. By giving them an assertive framework they will grow into assertive, confident people who like themselves and are liked by others. They will develop the self-discipline necessary to enable them to negotiate themselves through the education system and to make rational decisions when confronted with the many temptations of young life. They will also have the tools to seek out help and advice and maybe even offer it to others. Listen to them, get to know them, love them a lot, have fun with them and let them know you.

*Children are a poor man's gold*, treasure them and help them to develop the skills necessary to be a successful human being.

## CHAPTER 11 SUMMARY

*The path of least resistance rarely leads to happiness*

- Be assertive with yourself. Set your goals and stop putting things off.
- Be a person who does things, not a person who merely talks about doing things.

- If you are in a position of leadership then you have the responsibility to set out the rules and ensure that people comply with them.
- Nip things in the bud before they start to grow; people have the right to have their unacceptable behaviour pointed out to them in order that they have the opportunity to change.
- Parents are the grown-ups; it is their responsibility to develop discipline in their children.

## CHAPTER 12

# Steps to becoming more assertive

As stated earlier, it is wise to approach the skills of assertiveness fairly gradually. Using practice situations like the 'car boot' example in Chapter 3 will help to build your confidence where you have nothing to lose. The effect has a self-fulfilling pattern: **you become more assertive in these situations → your self-esteem increases → you become more confident → you behave more assertively** . . . and so it goes on. Furthermore, by thinking through situations, you actually become clearer about what you really do and don't want. You are more able to set goals based on how you would really like things to be rather than some vague notion that you don't like the way things are.

## WET KNOTS

We are complicated beings with a tendency to weave complicated relationships with people. Sometimes these relationships become so complex that trying to deal with them is rather like trying to untie a very tight, wet knot. Spending time giving constructive thought to this relationship can ensure that your motive and your approach to dealing with it are clear and specific.

*Write down a situation which you want to deal with assertively*:
THE SITUATION IS . . .


*Now write down how you actually feel about this*:
MY FEELINGS ARE . . .


*Now write down how you would like things to be – sometimes a useful question to ask yourself here is 'what would life be like if I didn't have this problem?'*
I WOULD LIKE . . .


After you have gone through this process it is essential to ask yourself DO I HAVE THE RIGHT?

– If the answer is YES then GO FOR IT!
– If the answer is NO then maybe you need to change your own attitude and make the best of the situation.


## NEXT STEPS

Plan how you are going to put your feelings across to the other person. Go back to the communication principles in Chapters 1 and 10 as a reminder and then do a bit of rehearsing. This may sound rather silly and contrived, but if it is important to you then you are worth it.

**Role play**
Explain to somebody who you trust what it is you are

trying to do. Brief them by describing the situation and the person you are going to be dealing with. Give some thought to setting the scene. Where will you be? Will you sit or stand? How are you going to open the conversation so that you have their attention? Go through the discussion, ensuring that you leave the other person knowing what you would like, whilst remembering the importance of listening to them. At the end of the discussion you can ask the person how they thought you came over, and also think about what you might do differently when it is 'the real thing'. Check out what they observed about your body language and your tone of voice.

## On Tape

Sit in a room with a tape recorder and talk through what you want to say. When you play it back, listen to *what* you say and *how* you say it. Do you sound assertive or might the other person think you are being aggressive? Pauses, frequent apologies, or an unspecific message will make it easy for the listener to dismiss what you are saying. Try putting yourself in their shoes. Does what you hear sound as though it will assertively achieve what you want?

## The Mirror

If you are aware that your body language sometimes lets you down, either because it suggests aggression or passiveness, then a good session in front of a full-length mirror can help. Pretend you are talking to somebody with whom you are trying to behave assertively. Stand with your weight evenly balanced, your shoulders back and head up. Let your arms hang loosely with your hands open and relaxed. Note where you feel any tension and try to relax that part of your body. How do you like yourself when you look assertive? I think you look great! Make your assertive statement to express what you would like.

Now, staying in front of the mirror, adopt a *passive* pose and try putting your point across.

Do you notice that your voice has softened and become more hesitant, in keeping with your body posture? You have probably put your weight onto one leg, hunched your shoulders slightly and clasped your hands in front of you.

Now adopt an *aggressive* pose and say the same thing.

What has happened to your voice? What is this likely to do to your listener? It will probably cause them to become defensive or to be aggressive back to you which means it is unlikely to result in a WIN/WIN outcome. In this instance you have probably put your weight onto one foot, are leaning forward slightly; maybe your hands are either on your hips or one is raised and pointing.

Don't forget, **you can choose**; think about the rainbow arc in Chapter 4. The situation or person you are dealing with might necessitate moderating your assertiveness either towards the *passive* or the *aggressive* end of the spectrum.

**Progress diary**
When you embark on any personal development it is useful to keep a log to record your progress. Write down what you have decided to become more assertive about, starting with little things and working up to the 'wet knots'. Then, after dealing with one of these, or any spontaneous situation, you can note down:

1.  HOW YOU HANDLED IT

2.  HOW YOU WOULD LIKE TO HAVE HANDLED IT
3.  WHAT YOU MIGHT DO DIFFERENTLY NEXT TIME

As you gain in confidence and skill you will find that there is little difference between 1 and 2, so that 3 merely becomes refinement of your skills.

**Self-assertion**
Unless you are in a position of advocacy – for a child, for a member of your staff or for somebody who is officially in your care – you should avoid being assertive on somebody else's behalf. Playing the 'rescuer' role can make you feel good, but it reinforces the other person's helplessness, depriving them of an opportunity to choose to be assertive for themselves. It can also be seen as aggressive by the person on the receiving end. By rescuing a 'victim' you are in danger of making somebody else a 'victim' of you.

**Lighten it with laughter**
Humour is such a useful vehicle for carrying heavy loads. In the attempt to be assertive it is sometimes easy to fall into a trap of becoming too serious. Remember: *angels fly high because they take themselves lightly*.

**Positive Outcomes**
In my dealings with Assertiveness Training I have encountered numerous 'success stories' of people who have gone through some of the *pain* to be rewarded with the *gain* of achieving greater self-respect through a more comfortable relationship with themselves and others. I thought it might be useful to include a few examples of these.

Anna is a graduate in her late twenties whose appearance is very feminine and dainty. Having failed to get any job in her qualified area she attended a series of seminars designed to help people to improve their career prospects through various aspects of jobsearch skills. She had succeeded in getting to the interview stage many times, but was never offered the job. The idea of 'selling herself' filled her with horror as she felt that she didn't want to become 'that sort of person'. She didn't like people who were assertive and neither did her boyfriend. She was clearly unhappy with her life as it was and decided not to close her mind completely during the sessions dealing with assertiveness. After a few weeks she wrote the following: '*My definition of assertiveness is the ability to believe in myself and to be able to communicate a point clearly, precisely and without being pushy or aggressive. It is also a way of being more at peace with myself – feeling that I don't have to validate all of my actions, just being able to explain them clearly if pushed.*' Of the next four jobs she was interviewed for, she was offered three.

Jean is a happy, generous woman who likes children and is always willing to help people out. She started reading about assertiveness and began putting some of the skills and ideas into practice. She describes how pleased she felt when her best friend said to her: '*The pity about you becoming more assertive is that I don't feel that I can dump my kids on you now. But I must say that I do like you more!*'

John is a quiet, thoughtful man who worked in a busy, changing office. He had been suffering stress and was sent for a short series of counselling sessions by his GP. It became clear that, apart from a heavy workload, he was suffering harassment from his predominantly female colleagues. The counsellor helped him to understand more about what was going on and the effect it was having on him. His determination not to let it get the better of him made him learn more about assertiveness. He wrote to the counsellor six months after they had ended their sessions to say that *'I went back into work with my head up and shoulders back. Although I felt like jelly inside I kept my voice steady and controlled. At the first sign of [their] unacceptable behaviour I told them that I wasn't willing to put up with it and that I thought we could improve our working relationship by behaving in a more adult way. Although there was quite a lot of tension in the office for a few days it settled down and we just get on with the work now. It's such a relief not dreading going into work each day, I think I've probably "lightened up" a bit and maybe I'm easier to get along with.'*

## YOUR TURN

I now invite you to write your own 'success story' – you may choose to do one or both of these now or at a later date.

1. Whilst reading this book I have put some of the learning into practice with the following result . . .


2. Because of what I now intend to do, by [date —] my success story will read . . .


The list below represents some more general things which people say they are going to do in order to improve their assertiveness:

Confront problems, not run away from them
Say 'No' when appropriate
Express my feelings
Be realistic about what I can and can't do
Write my own Bill of Rights
Address problems before they become BIG
Take responsibility for myself
Encourage others to be assertive
Move on, let some of the past go
Be a better friend to myself
Stay calm
Be positive
Be specific
Evaluate situations
Like myself more
Not to be put upon
Think *I'm OK – You're OK*
Accept my mistakes
Be more direct

*Go back through this list, tick any which you WILL do and add more of your own.*

**In each case ask yourself:**
– WILL I?
– WHEN?
– HOW?
– WHAT WILL THE BENEFIT BE TO ME?
– WILL ANYBODY ELSE BENEFIT?

Finally . . . however good you become at assertiveness the only person you can be in control of is yourself. We don't have control over what somebody else thinks, feels or believes, although we can hope that in some small way we might influence them. What you can control totally is what **you** think, feel and believe. Admittedly this is very grown-up, as it doesn't allow any hiding places where we can deposit blame or responsibility on others, but there is a wonderful liberation in this as it gives us total control over how we *choose* to behave. Taking responsibility for yourself allows you to be yourself so that *you are the driver, not the passenger, in your life's journey*. As you continue through your journey don't forget to be kind, forgiving, tolerant and loving towards yourself. Growing and learning is part of life's richness; *personal development is a journey, not a destination*. Make sure you are a good travelling companion for yourself – remember to forgive yourself if you get it wrong and to celebrate when you get it right.

# FREE PERSONAL TRAINER SESSION

## with *Fitness First*

If you're looking to improve your motivation and need a change to your current gym routine, look no further! Here's the perfect offer to boost your energy levels and give your fitness regime a kick-start!

You can book a free personal trainer session with one of the participating *Fitness First* venues. To take up this offer simply cut out the token overleaf and send it with your till receipt and a stamped self-addressed envelope to **Perfect Series Personal Trainer Session offer**, MKM House, Manchester M16 0XX. You will be sent a Personal Trainer voucher plus a list of participating venues. Call the venue closest in your area to arrange a suitable date and time. When calling the venue state that you hold a **Free Personal Trainer Voucher**. You *Fitness First* personal trainer will give you a **Free** consultation, and a $1\frac{1}{2}$ hour session focusing on your own personal goals, combined with a free day pass allowing access to the club facilities.

## HAPPY TRAINING!

*Fitness First* is also offering a fantastic discount on membership. Save £5 each month when you join as a 'Gold' member for just £29 per month outside of London and £39 per month within London. 'Gold' membership will allow you to use the great facilities at *Fitness First* all year round.

All associated joining and administration fees will apply.

If you have any queries or require further information regarding this offer, please call our Helpline on 0161 877 1113. (Lines open Mon-Fri 9am-5.30pm, calls charged at standard rate)

SEE OVER FOR TERMS AND CONDITIONS AND TOKEN

# FREE PERSONAL TRAINER SESSION

## with *FitnessFirst*

Get fit with a private consultation from one of *FitnessFirst*'s specially selected personal trainers

Claim by 31.12.03. Voucher valid until 31.03.04 See below for terms and conditions.

Cash redemption value 0.01p

## TERMS AND CONDITIONS

1. Offer open to all residents over 18 in the UK and Republic of Ireland. 2. One **Free Personal Trainer voucher** entitles the bearer to one free session with a personal trainer. The session will take place at the *FitnessFirst* health club where the participating personal trainer is based. The voucher also entitles the bearer to the use of the fitness and leisure facilities on the day the session is booked. Be aware that facilities differ from club to club, although most venues offer free use of the gym and pool. 3. The discounted membership offer allows customers to save £5 per month when applying for a 'Gold' membership. You can become a Gold member for just £29 per month outside of London and £39 per month within London. All associated joining and administration fees apply. 4. The voucher is valid for use until 31.03.04 Certain date restrictions may apply; these can be verified with the *FitnessFirst* venue of your choice. 5. Original vouchers only. 6. Your free session has to be booked in advance. 7. The **Personal Trainer voucher** cannot be used in conjunction with any other promotion or offer. 8. One person may book one session with a participating trainer on one occasion only. 9. Standard terms and conditions of personal trainer sessions apply and are available at each *FitnessFirst* venue. 10. Customers may be required to complete a health and fitness form before beginning training. 11. The Promoter and MKM can accept no liability for personal loss or injury in any session with a personal trainer, as far as permitted by law. 12. The cash redemption value of each voucher is 0.01p, and no alternative will be offered. This promotion is administered on behalf of the promoter Random House, 20 Vauxhall Bridge Road, London, SW1V 2SA by MKM Marketing & Promotions Ltd, Manchester M16 0XX. If you have any queries, or require further information on this offer, please call our HELPLINE on 0161 877 1113. (Lines open from Mon-Fri 9am-5.30pm calls charged at standard rates)